Thy Ki

Thy Kingdom Come

The Kingdom of God Now and Forever

by

Dr. Kirby Clements Sr.

CLEMENTS
MINISTRIES

Decatur, GA

Thy Kingdom Come: The Kingdom of God Now and Forever

Address inquiries to the publisher:
Clements Family Ministries
2000 Cathedral Place
Decatur, Georgia 30034 USA

Learn more about the author and the ministry at www.clementsministries.org

ISBN: 978-0-9794181-6-7 (print)
ISBN: 978-0-9794181-9-8 (ebook)

Library of Congress Control Number: 2015954159

Edited and composed by Annette Johnson, Allwrite Communications Inc.
Cover by Melissa Phillips

Printed in the United States of America.

Table of Contents

Dedication

To my daughter, Gina, who insists that there is always a right way.

Acknowledgments

The ministry of Bishop Earl Paulk is the central focus in this book. His willingness to proclaim the power, principles, and strategies of the Kingdom of God at a local church level is the single most important factor in the origination of this project.

Preface

The relationship between faith, conviction, and behavior is quite well established. It is a well-tested proposition that individual and corporate decisions, attitudes, values, and judgments hinge upon some form of a belief system. The belief system is usually the product of knowledge and wisdom gained through personal experiences and relationships in the natural and spiritual environment. Moments of discovery occur when the natural world of people, words, ideas, and events presents new information. There are also those instances when the spiritual world of dreams, prophecies, revelations, and intuitions reveals insight, knowledge, wisdom, and understanding. When the source and the content of such information is accepted as truth, then there comes a time when these words, ideas, symbols, types, shadows, pictures, prophecies, dreams, revelations, and beliefs are put into action.

In this work, there is an effort to explore the relationship that exists between the conception of the Kingdom of God and the attitude and behavior of the redeemed community. Perception is everything. The belief that God is the Creator, Organizer, and Maintainer of all things; that He is involved in human affairs; that He has made known His purposes and intentions; and that there can be an acceptable human response to such knowledge should influence the objectives and priorities of the redeemed community in its stewardship responsibilities of the earth. Redeemed humanity, as vice-regents or earthly representatives of God, is called to disciple nations and reconcile the world unto God. The world represents humanity estranged from God; it is humanity with all of its devices, schemes, institutions, and knowledge seeking to govern itself without God. The attitude of the redeemed community toward the world in its state of "lostness" is greatly influenced by its conception or misconception of the Kingdom of God.

The Kingdom of God, with all of its principles and power, is the interpretative concept that defines reality, value, authority, righteousness, justice, joy, and even evil. After all, what is real and what is important? Who is in charge? What is the right way? And what is evil and how powerful is its influence? The conception or the misconception of the Kingdom of God determines the answers.

Jesus and the Kingdom of God are distinct but inseparable. It is Jesus, the King of God's Kingdom, who defines the Kingdom and demonstrates its principles and its power. For that reason, much of our knowledge and understanding of the Kingdom of God is derived from the teachings of Jesus as reported in the Gospels and in the writings of the apostles. The idea of the Kingdom is a consistent theme throughout the Scriptures with diversities of meanings and applications. It is the manifested expression of the sovereignty of God as Creator, Organizer, and Maintainer of all creation. It is everlasting and endures throughout all generations. It is not a philosophy of words or ideas, but it is active power. It is the manifestation of divine authority over evil forces. It is power to influence and transform nations. In principle, practice, value, and judgment, it stands apart from the systems, organizations, institutions, and distortions of this present world. It is not defined by human preferences or cultural values or attitudes, but it is "righteousness, peace, and joy in the Holy Spirit." A "born again" individual can see it and enter into it. Yet, there are some individuals who cannot inherit it. It is not restricted to some geographic location, time, or season. It is present and future; heavenly and earthly; spiritual and natural; and divine and human. When it is preached, accepted, and demonstrated, it transforms lives and nations.

The source and the authority of our topic, Kingdom of God, is supernatural, yet it has tremendous natural implications. It will become obvious in this study that there is hardly any subject in the whole field of New Testament research that provokes greater diversity of opinions or gives rise to as much controversy as the Kingdom of God. All factions agree on its existence but disagree on its nature and implications. Views range from a future hope, present spiritual blessing, an alternative society, a Utopian existence, the institutional church, to a political state. With such a diversity of opinions there arises the possibility that the Kingdom may serve as the focal point of unity and disunity. And if God's Kingdom presents the opportunity for a variety of interpretations and if these diverse opinions are only a partial view of the whole picture, then the nature, power, and implication of the Kingdom become the focal point of both unity and diversity. If this principle of unity and diversity is accepted, then the Kingdom of God is the focal point. In this work, we wish to examine this possibility while exploring the implications of the Kingdom of God upon the identity and ministry of the Church.

—*Kirby Clements Sr.*

CHAPTER 1

Idea of The Kingdom

When we pray, "Thy Kingdom come; Thy will be done in earth as it is in heaven," according to Matt. 6:10, we are asking for trouble. We are requesting light to collide with darkness, and truth to invalidate error. In essence, we are asking for God to impose or apply His everlasting Kingdom principles to our current earthly state. This request may conjure a cataclysmic shift in a believer's perception or experiences.

Mary and Joseph went to Bethlehem, according to God's will, but they had no place to stay when they arrived. Thus, the pregnant Mary had to deliver the baby, Christ, in a stable. In obeying God's will, they experienced personal rejection and discomfort, but they gained spiritual redemption and eternal life – for themselves and for all those who would believe that *the* King was born in that stable.

Who would intentionally ask for radical change that may separate someone from his or her passions, views and lifestyle? Who would ask for possible discomfort and rejection? This is what we pray for when we say we want to yield to the implications and outcomes of Kingdom rule.

"Thy Kingdom come" represents a desire for the coming fulfillment of God's recreation of humanity. The phrase "Thy will be done" represents an immediate desire for the fulfillment of God's perfect order. In other words, the entire statement denotes the idea or concept of the Kingdom: God's rule now and forever.

An Enduring Central Theme

It may be said that the entire preaching of Jesus Christ and His apostles is the Kingdom of God, and in the preaching of the Kingdom, we are brought face to face with the whole revelation of God. If this statement is true, then we are not thinking and preaching correctly if we are not focusing on the Kingdom of God.

The Kingdom of God is not an optional point of reference; it is *the* essential reference. It is the manifested rule and the expressed sovereignty of God, and it is separate and distinct from any earthly ideology, philosophy, system, structure, organization, or form of government. The principles and the power of the Kingdom of God are eternal and applicable to every generation, people, nation, and world.

It is perhaps for this reason that there is hardly any subject in the whole field of New Testament research that provokes greater diversity of opinions or gives rise to as much controversy (discussed in Chapter 8). Opinions range from the view of a future hope (John 18:36), present spiritual blessing (Luke 6:20), an alternative society (Luke 17:20-21), a Utopian existence (Rev. 21-22), the institutional church (Matt. 16:19), to a political state (Matt. 13:31-34). Part of the reason for such diversity of opinions is due to efforts to detach the conception of the Kingdom of God from its historical background (1 Chr. 29:11-13; Psalm 10:15; 103:19; 145:11; 146:11-13; Isaiah 37:16). For example, the opening of the New Testament begins with the message of John Baptist: "Repent, for the kingdom of heaven is at hand" (Matt. 3:2). Jesus preaches the Kingdom; trains His disciples in the message; and includes it as an essential ingredient in prayer (Matt.3:l-2; 4:17,23; 6:33; 9:35; 24:14; Mark 1:14,15; 4:11; 9:47; 10:14-25; Luke 4:23; 6:20; 9:11; 11:20; 12:31; 16:16; 17:20-21; 18:16-29; John 3:3,5; 18:36). The Kingdom is a post-resurrection message of Jesus for 40 days (Acts 1:2-3).

The book of Acts includes the preaching of the Kingdom of God (Acts 8:12; 20:25-27). At the close of Acts, Paul is preaching the Kingdom of God (Acts 28:30-31). Finally, the language of the Kingdom appears nine times in seven letters indicating its relation to Christian conduct and its significance to those redeemed everywhere (Rom. 14:17; 1 Cor. 4:20; 6:9; Gal. 5:19-21; Eph. 5:5; Col. 1:13-14; 1 Thess. 2:12; 2 Thess. 1:5).

Paul presents three dimensions of the Kingdom as past, present, and future (Rom. 14-17; 1 Cor. 15:24, 50; Gal. 5:21; Eph. 5:5; Col. 1:13; 4:11; 2 Thess. 1:5). The Kingdom is come in the incarnation, life, ministry, death, and resurrection of Jesus Christ the King. The Kingdom is here as an experience in the Holy Ghost, its gifts, fruits, and the struggles against "the flesh" and "the world;" and the Kingdom is coming with the Second Coming of Christ when "God will be all in all" (1 Cor. 15:28).

Although the phrase "Kingdom of God" is not a standard expression in the Old Testament as it is in the New Testament, there are some passages that contain the equivalent of the dominion of God:

> *For the kingdom is the Lord's, and He rules over the nations.* (Psalm 22:28)

> *The Lord has established His throne in heaven, and His kingdom rules over all.* (Psalm 103:19)

> *The Lord is high above all nations, and His glory above the heavens.* (Psalm 113:4)

> *They shall speak of the glory of Your kingdom, and talk of Your power.* (Psalm 145:11)

> *How great are his signs! And how mighty are his wonders! His kingdom is an everlasting kingdom, and his dominion is from generation to generation.* (Daniel 4:3)

> *And it shall come to pass in the last days that the mountain of the Lord's house shall be established in the top of the mountains, and shall be exalted above the hills; and all nations shall flow into it.* (Isaiah 2:2)

The idea of the Kingdom of God is a connection between the Old and the New Testament. It is the reality of the sovereign rule of God demonstrated in earthly affairs that is evident in both the old and the new covenant. The fact that the rule of God is eternal without restriction of time or geography (Hab. 2:14; John 4:21-24); that the truths of this Kingdom endure throughout every generation regardless of the century (Dan. 2:34; Psalm 118:22-23; Matt. 21:42); that the expectation of Old Testament prophets find fulfillment with the New Testament apostles and prophets (Amos 9:13, 14; Isaiah 2:2, 4; 9:7; 11:1,9; 25:8; 40:5; 49:5; Jer. 23:5; Joel 2:28-32; Matt. 1:15; Luke 16:16 Acts 2:16-21; 3:18; 26:6,7; Eph. 3:1-6; 1 Pet. 1:10-12); and that what is once declared to be a mystery becomes very clear (Gen. 12:3; 1 Cor. 12:13; Gal. 3:6-9; 6:15; Eph. 3:1-9; Col. 1:26-27), is the association between the old and the new. What holy men of old did testify, without understanding, concerning the coming of the Lord (1 Pet. 1:10-12), a later generation of apostles and prophets preach with clarity and demonstrate its power and implications (Acts 2:16-39; 10:34-43; 15:1-18; Eph. 3:1-12).

Kingdom Principles

The idea of the rule of God in every generation is expressed in the presence and continuance of irrevocable norms and core values for all areas of life, people, and nations (Psalm 100:5; 1 Pet. 1:25). These principles of the Kingdom serve as guidelines to preserve the humanity and dignity of the citizens under divine rule. These irrevocable norms and core values that are presented in the Law, the Prophets, and the ethical teachings of Jesus and the apostles are an exposition of the ethics of the Kingdom of God. They indicate that the truths of God endure throughout every generation.

As members of the Kingdom, we live according to certain immutable principles that have been declared through the Word of God:

Privilege – promise to grant us anything we ask in faith through prayer unless it violates the nature, character, doctrine or will of God (Matt. 13:58, 15:21-28, 17:20; Mark 9:23, 11:23; John 5:14, 15:7; James 1:5-8, 5:14-18)

Provision – promise to always provide for His children just as He has for the birds in the sky (Matt. 6:25-26, 33; Luke 5:1-7)

Power – provide the Spirit as power to those who believe (John 14:15-17; Acts 1:4-5, 2:1-4, 33)

Promises of Righteousness, Peace and Joy – provided as fruit of the Spirit, not fruit of the ground or human effort (Rom.14:17)

Planting and Reaping – principle of reciprocity is based on the motives of our thoughts and actions (Gen. 1:11-12; Mal. 3:10; Mark 4:1-34; Luke 6:38)

Promotion – provided to those who are the greatest servants, not the greatest leaders (Matt. 18:1-4; Luke 14:11)

The Kingdom has one law: **love**, which should be expressed in sincerely loving God and others (Matt. 22:36-40; Mark 12:30-31). The values and lifestyle of the Kingdom of God are opposite of those in the kingdoms of this world, which include:

*   The world says, *"Certain things are unforgivable."*
    The Kingdom says, *"Repent, and turn or return to God."*
    (Matt. 3:2, 4:17; Luke 15:1-7; 8-10, 11-32)

*   The world says, *"Get revenge."*
    The Kingdom says, *"Turn the other cheek and do good to those who mistreat you."* (Prov. 25:21-22; Matt. 5:38-41; Rom 12:17-21)

*   The world says, *"Hate your enemies."*
    The Kingdom says, *"Love your enemies."* (Matt. 5:43-48)

*   The world says, *"Take what you can or what you deserve."*
    The Kingdom says, *"Give and it will be given back to you."*
    (Matt. 6:1-4; Luke 6:38)

*   The world says, *"Seek prosperity on earth."*
    The Kingdom says, *"Focus on prosperity in heaven."*
    (Matt. 6:19-21)

* The world says, *"There are many paths to God."*
  The Kingdom says, *"Jesus is the only way, the truth and the life."*
  (Matt. 7:13; John 14:6; 2 Cor. 5:21)

* The world says, *"Preserve your life at all costs."*
  The Kingdom says, *"Lose your life and you will find it."*
  (Matt. 10:39, 16:25; Luke 9:24, 17:33)s

* The world says, *"Be proud and assertive if you want to become great."*
  The Kingdom says, *"Serve and be humble if you want to be great."*
  (Matt. 23:11-12)

The idea of the Kingdom of God is the existence of Divine rule, order, and purposes in the earthly affairs of believers throughout every generation. It is the fact that God is involved in human affairs; that His intentions and purposes for all creation is made known; and that human response to the revelation of this knowledge is made possible. The Kingdom is a God idea in the sense that it is not defined by any earthly ideology, philosophy, system, structure, organization, or form of government. This is a prevalent theme throughout the Biblical record and is the central idea in the preaching of Jesus and the apostles.[1]

---

1   Howard A. Snyder, Models of the Kingdom (Nashville, Term.: Abingdon Press, 1991), 18.

Foundation of The Kingdom

The creation motif is the basis for the government of God (Gen. 1-3; Acts 17:24-31). God creates time, space, material, and people. This is difficult to understand since we neither have eyewitnesses nor is there any parallel to describe God prior to creation. For example, we say God resides in heaven, yet in the beginning, He creates the very place of His residence (heaven) and earth. So where was He in the beginning? He comes out of His "where-ever-ness" or "what-ever-ness" to create. He is the Alpha (beginning) and Omega (ending). He has no beginning or ending in His essence, but He does in terms of His involvement in a world organized in time and space. On the basis of God as Creator rests the entire concept of His unlimited dominion and rule, for "the earth is the Lord's and all its fullness" (Psalm 24:1). It is the basis of all revelation of God as Ruler, Organizer, and Maintainer of all creation.

In the Scripture, creation, not evolution, is clearly established as fact (Gen. 1-2; Exodus 20:11; Psalm 24:1; 90:2; Isaiah 45:7, 12; Jer. 27:5; Acts 17:24-26; Rom. 1:20; 11:36; Rev. 14:7). It is God who creates all things, principalities, and powers (Prov. 16:4; 22:2; 26:10; Rom. 9:17). He determines the purpose, organization, and ongoing function of all creation

(Psalm 74:16; Neh. 9:6; Acts 17:24-26). There is a tendency to confuse the progressive revelation of Divine purposes and intentions with the process of evolution. This occurs because we have nothing to compare the fact that God creates time, space, material purposes, functions, and gives a sequence to the human understanding of this process. That is, whether the progression of life is from the one (Adam) to the many (nations) or from the simple to the complex, it is God who is the Creator of all. It must be understood that the Bible is not a book of science or anthropology, but it is the revelation of God and His involvement with His creation.

In creation, God materializes His image in mankind, establishes a covenant, and delegates authority (Gen. 1:26-28; 2:7-24; Psalm 8:4-8). This Creator/creature relationship clearly establishes the unilateral right of God to exercise His thoughts, purposes, and plans. It also indicates that the creatures and all creation are in subjection to God. His intention in creating Adam (male and female) is that they should multiply, fill the earth, subdue it and bring all things under the government of God. The limited or jurisdictional authority of mankind is defined by these Divine purposes and intentions. Hence, in creation there is a moral obligation of mankind to the Creator. This moral obligation is expressed in mankind's delegated stewardship of the earth with all of the privileges, provisions, promises, responsibilities and restrictions (Gen. 2:15-25). God never indicates that He will be passive or uninvolved with mankind or the creation (Gen. 3:8-24). We will discuss this idea later when we examine concepts of a worldview.

God creates all nations and gives angelic oversight over them (Gen. 9:18, 10:5, 20, 31,32; Job 12:23; Psalm 22:28, 66:7, 67:4, 82:8, 86:9; 103:19, 145:11, Acts 17:26). Nations are sociological units created by God to compartmentalize humanity into manageable forms. The purpose for their existence is not to glorify their human differences but to seek after God and glorify Him. The management of these units or nations is through the providential rule of God. For example, when nations rebel against the Lord, there are environmental consequences that are dictated by His providence. Productivity is devoured (Deut. 28:15-26); disease is rampant (Deut. 28:27); economic and political depression occurs (Deut. 28:28-34). For the obedient nations, the desert is transformed into an oasis (Isaiah 35, 43:19-21) and physical, material, political, and economic blessings flow (Isaiah 32:15-16). Spiritual blindness is the consequence of sustained rebellion against the Lord (Psalm 1:4-6; Rom. 1:21-31; 2 Thess. 2:10-12).

However, to the obedient there is spiritual enlightenment, which contributes to creativity and productivity in every sphere of human involvement (Psalm 1:1-3). Material and spiritual blessings relate directly to cultural obedience.

The purpose and power of the Kingdom find expression in several Old Testament passages:

> *Ask of me and I shall give thee the heathens for thine inheritance; and the uttermost parts of the earth for thy possession.* (Psalm 2:8)

> *For the Kingdom is the Lord's and He rules over the nations.* (Psalm 22:28)

> *He rules by His might forever; His eyes keep watch over the nations.* (Psalm 66:7)

> *Let the nations be glad...for thou will govern the nations of the earth.* (Psalm 67:4)

> *He shall have dominion from sea to sea and from the River to the ends of the earth.* (Psalm 72:8)

> *Yes, all kings shall fall down before Him; all nations shall fall down before Him.* (Psalm 72:11)

All authority comes from God (Rom. 13:1), even Satanic authority (Job 2). God's appointed leaders are well aware of this fact. Note the prayers of Hezekiah and David, respectively:

> *O Lord, God of Israel, which dwellest between the cherubim, thou are the God, even thou alone, of all the kingdoms of the earth; thou hast made heaven and earth.* (2 Kings 19:15)

> *Thine, O Lord is the greatness, and the power, and the glory, and the victory, and the majesty for all that is in the heaven and in the earth is thine; thine is the kingdom,*

O Lord, and thou art exalted as head of all. Both riches
and honor come of thee, and thou reignest over all; and in
thine hand it is to make great, and to give strength unto all.
(1 Chronicles 29:11-12)

Hence, the Kingdom of God is the sovereign reign and manifest priority of God. This authority is delegated in part to humanity (Gen. 1:28; Luke 19:13; Matt. 28:19-20; Mark 16:15). That is, the revelation of the righteousness of God may be expressed in human government and in the management of all earthly affairs. Although this is not always done, God still imparts concepts of righteousness that may be demonstrated in institutions, organizations, and systems of human expressions such as economics, politics, commerce, science, entertainment, athletics, and so forth. This is the meaning that is to be ascribed to such concepts as dominion (Gen. 1:28), occupy (Luke 19:13), and make disciples of all nations (Matt. 28:19-20; Mark 16:15). This demonstrates that the Kingdom of God is not restricted to religious matters but involves all areas of human existence.

The Impact of Sin

As aforementioned, creation is the foundation of this reality of God's sovereign rule and authority. Mankind is created in the image of God and is equipped with the capacities of rationality, creativity, righteousness, and the power to rule over created things. Mankind is not constituted to rule apart from God. In fact, the major cause of disunity, disorder, disorientation, disease, disaster, and distress in the world is due to fallen humanity seeking to govern itself without the counsel of God. After creation, mankind forfeits the authority given and falls into judgment (Gen. 1-3). This original disobedience to Divine covenant introduces sin into the created order and that sin is comprehensive and progressive (Rom. 5:12-19). And so as it is recorded, "through one man's offense judgment came to all men, resulting in condemnation" and "by one man's disobedience many were made sinners" (Rom. 5:18-19). From Adam to Cain's murder, there is the progressive disorganization and disorientation of creation attempting to exist without the government of God. For this reason, all creation groans because it is subjected to the consequences of sin (Rom. 8:22). The end result of such rebellion is seen in the murder, division, wars, and all the activities of Satan to deceive, kill, steal, and destroy. It is the foundation behind all efforts of annihilation of entire nations and the crimes against humanity. Hence, the cause of disorganization in the beginning is believing Satan's lie and establishing an independent government apart from God.

However, it is also written that "through one Man's righteous act the free gift came to all men, resulting in justification of life" and "by one Man's obedience many will be made righteous" (Rom. 5:18-19). God begins a program for fallen humanity that involves the restructuring of human thought and behavior. This is the protocol and it involves redemption, re-generation, and restructure. Most Christians believe in regeneration, and going to heaven, but they fall short of the strategy for restructuring through a redeemed, Spirit-filled community that is organized by Divine principles: the Church. The prayer of the Lord Jesus is that "thy kingdom come, thy will be done on earth as it is in heaven" (Matt. 6:10). The reconstruction of Divine order on earth begins with the Church. The language of restruc-turing is to found in the biblical concept of history (Acts 17:24-31). As aforementioned, that by one man sin entered and that sin is comprehen-sive (individual and cosmic) and progressive (all generations), then by the obedience of one man redemption, regeneration, and restoration begins. As Adam is a type for the procreation of the human race, Jesus Christ is the Creator, Ruler, Organizer, and Maintainer of a whole new creation. The Church is His ongoing incarnation, and therefore, those who must carry out the total restoration.

Sin is comprehensive in its domain and affects the spirit, soul, and body of mankind and also the entire creation (Gen. 3:14-19; Rom. 8:19-22). Salvation is more comprehensive in reversing the affects of sin, for it is the revelation and the restoration of Divine purposes, authority, and order (John 3:16-17; 1 Cor. 15:20-28; 1 John 3:8). Since mankind never achieves Divine purposes and intentions prior to the coming of the Lord Jesus, it may be said that salvation is ultimate fulfillment and not only res-toration. Salvation materializes the formation of a "new heavens and new earth" in which righteousness dwells (2 Pet. 3:13). This fulfillment (resto-ration) of Divine purposes, authority, and order does not come through the literal annihilation of the entire planet (Gen. 9:8-17), but through the influential activities of the Holy Spirit working through an inspired, theo-logically informed, and obedient redeemed community. The tabernacle of God is among people, and redeemed humanity now has access to the

Father through the Son. Through the power of the Holy Spirit, divine ideas, concepts, programs, and strategies are imparted to redeemed humanity that serve as the foundation for institutions, organizations, policies, laws, governments, and relationships. This is the foundation of the Kingdom of God.

The Holy Spirit and the Kingdom

In creation, it is the power of the Spirit acting in response to the Word that facilitates the process (Gen. 1:1-23). This initial display of the power of the Holy Spirit finds a parallel in the statement by Paul that "the Kingdom of God is not food and drink, but righteousness and peace and joy in the Holy Spirit" (Rom. 14:17). This establishes an inseparable relationship between the Kingdom of God and the Holy Spirit. In fact, it can be said that the Kingdom is in the Holy Spirit.

While the creation motif is the foundation of the Kingdom, the Holy Spirit is the power.

As such, the Holy Spirit is the executive administrator of the creation, organization, and maintenance of all things (Luke 11:20; Acts 1:8; 17:24; Rom. 15:18-20; 1 Cor. 4:20; Heb. 1:3). It is the mission of the Spirit to bring to pass all the fruits of Christ's victory including the lordship over all things (Acts 2:34-35; 3:19-21; Eph. 1:10; 4:10). In salvation, it is the work of the Spirit that brings the sinner into covenant with God (John 3:3, 5; 14:23-26; 1 Cor. 12:3, 13). In fact, entrance into the Kingdom is brought about by the Spirit (John 3:5; 1 Cor. 12:13; 15:50).

The Holy Spirit regenerates the sinner and makes possible a faith response to the Word of God (Acts 1:8; 2:28-39; 1 Cor. 2: 4-16). He illuminates the mind of the believer with knowledge (Rom. 1:21; 2 Cor. 4:4; Eph. 5:8; 1 Cor. 2:14). Although the intelligence of the believer is influenced by the Holy Spirit, it is not informed intellectually (Rom. 12:2; Eph. 4:23). The Holy Spirit guides a renewal of the mind making it possible to receive insight not available to the unrenewed mind (1 Cor. 2:14; 16). It is the Word that contains the intelligence (Acts 4:33; 8:5-12; Rom. 10:1-17). In fact, the ministry of the Spirit and the Word are indispensable for conversion, growth, and maturity of the believer. Hence, it is important that there be a marriage between the power and the intelligence of the Kingdom. For power without intelligence breeds fanaticism and intelligence without power is simply intellectualism.

As aforementioned, the Holy Spirit is the executive administrator of the Kingdom (Mark 16:15-18; Luke 24:49; Acts 1:4-8). This is seen as the Spirit:

Guides (John 16:13; James 1:5)
Teaches (John 14:26; 1 Cor. 2:7-13)
Heals (1 Cor. 12:9), delivers (2 Cor. 4:8-18)
Restores (2 Cor. 12:7-9)
Enables the believer (John 14:16, 17; Rom. 8:26-27)

This work is also seen as the Spirit is involved in:

discipleship (John 14:25-26; 15:26-27; 16:12-15);
commission (John 20:19-23);
diaconate (Acts 6:3-5);
evangelism (Acts 8:15-17; 8:29-39; 9:17; 10:19, 44-47);
adjusting prejudice (Acts 11:12-17);
prophetic warnings (Acts 11:28, 20:22-24);
dealing with opposition (Acts 13:9);
validating ministry (Acts 4:33, 15:7-9; 2 Cor. 12:12);
ministerial directions (Acts 16:6-7);
facilitating transition (Acts 15:28-29);
preparing for persecution (Acts 20:22-23, 21:4-11); and
validating callings (Acts 20:28; 2 Cor. 13:3).

When other apostles and elders question the ministry of Peter, Paul, and Barnabas, it is the work of the Holy Spirit that settles the matter (Acts 11:1-18; 15:1-28).

CHAPTER 3

Dimensions of The Kingdom

As we expand on the idea and the reality of the Kingdom of God, we must understand both its redemptive and providential dimensions. In the days of the Reformers, people were aware of God in providence. In the last century, people became very redemptive-minded and lost sight of God in providence. Today, there is a decline of the awareness of the providence of God in contemporary religious thinking. While the salvation of the individual may be the center of God's will, it is not the circumference (Psalm 10:15; 29:10; 103:19; 145:1-13; 146:10). God rules over the kingdom of men and determines the boundaries of their habitation (Gen. 9:32; 10:1-9; Dan. 4:7; 5:21-22; 11:34, 35, 44, 45; Psalm 24:1; 86:9; Acts 17:24-31). God is king at all times, seasons, events, and circumstances. It is the testimony of Scripture that "He put all things under His feet, and gave Him to be the head over all things" and His fullness is to fill all things (Eph. 1:22). He rules in the affairs of the universe and not simply among Christians. Failure to comprehend this dimension of the Kingdom of God results in a preoccupation with the redemptive dimension of God (individual salvation) at the expense of the knowledge and implication of God's role in the affairs of the universe (cosmic salvation).

The providence of God exerts a moral influence over the agents of earthly government according to His design. As already mentioned, the right of mankind to govern implies obligation to the moral and ethical demands of the Creator. Notice the following references:

> *The God of Israel said, the Rock of Israel spoke to me. He that ruleth over men must be just, ruling in the fear of God.* (2 Samuel 23:3)

> *And the Lord hardened the heart of Pharaoh…and in every deed for this cause have I raised thee up for to shew in thee my power and that my name may be declared throughout all the earth.* (Exodus 9:12-16)

> *Remember the former things of old; for I am God, and there is none else; I am God, and there is none like me. Declaring the end from the beginning, and from ancient times the things that are not yet done, and I will do all my pleasure. Calling a ravenous bird from the east, the man that executeth my counsel from a far country; yea, I have spoken it, I will also bring it to past; I have purposed it, I will also do it.* (Isaiah 46:9-11)

> *He hath shewed thee, O man, what is good; and what doth the Lord require of thee, but to do justly, and to love mercy, and to walk humbly with thy God.* (Micah 6:8)

> *This matter is by the decree of the watchers, and the demand by the word of the holy ones; to the intent that the living may know that the most High ruleth in the kingdom of men, and giveth it to whomsoever he will, and setteth up over it the basest of men.* (Daniel 4:17-18)

> *I Nebuchadnezzar lifted up mine eyes unto heaven, and mine understanding returned unto me, and I blessed the most High, and I praised and honored him that liveth for ever; whose dominion is an everlasting dominion, and his kingdom is from generation to generation; and all the inhabitants of the earth are reputed as nothing;*

and he doeth according to his will in the army of heaven, and among the inhabitants of the earth; and none can stay his hand, or say unto him, What doest thou? (Daniel 4:34-35)

Let every soul be subject unto the higher powers. For there is no power but of God, the powers that be are ordained of God: and they that resist shall receive to themselves damnation. For rulers are not a terror to good works but to the evil. Wilt thou then not be afraid of the power? Do that which is good, and thou shalt have praise of the same; for he is the minister of God to thee for good. But if thou do that which evil, be afraid; for he beareth not the sword in vain; for he is the minister of God, a revenger to execute wrath upon him that doeth evil. Wherefore ye must needs be subject, not only for wrath but also for conscience's sake. For, for this cause pay ye tribute also; for they are God's ministers, attending continually upon this very thing. Render, therefore, to all their dues; tribute to whom tribute is due; custom to whom custom; fear to whom fear; honor to whom honor. (Romans 13:1-7)

It must be understood that God is king over angels (Gen. 32:1, 2; Josh. 1:11; Psalm 103:19-22; Jer. 46:18). He is king over and during all times and events (Psalm 10:16, 29:10, 145:1-13, 146:10; Jer. 10:10). Daniel records that "He changeth the times and the seasons; He removeth kings, and setteth up kings; He giveth wisdom unto the wise, and knowledge to them that know understanding" (Dan. 2:21). There must be a reawakening to the rule of God not only in redemption of the individual, but also in the providential rule of all creation.

This principle is displayed through Jeremiah the prophet. The Lord delegates Jeremiah as the "overseer" or bishop over the nations (Jer. 1:4-10). During this time, there are many nations, kings, and rulers who do no know Jeremiah. Nevertheless, Jeremiah's authority is not based upon his friendship with earthly governmental powers but upon God delegated authority. The ultimate importance of Jeremiah is not that nations, kings, and rulers know him but that God knows him. Jeremiah will have the word of God channeled through him. The nations are ultimately subject to the predictive, ethical, redemptive, and judgmental word of God delegated by the prophet.

This concept seems foreign to the natural mind because as natural people we are impressed with human authority, armies, buildings, and the things we comprehend with our senses (1 Cor. 2:2-16). This principle is displayed in the account of Elisha and the Syrian war, in which it is revealed that the unseen forces are greater in number and power than the visible armies of men (2 Kings 6:8-17). We neglect to comprehend that the things that are seen are temporal and shall pass away, while the things that are unseen are eternal. The display of human authority is nothing in comparison to the authority of God. Faith comprehends this fact while unbelief refuses to accept it. The fact that in the beginning of time, the earth is created, organized, and maintained by the Word of God and the same Word of God is entrusted to delegated servants who oversee nations is still a faith proposition. We must remember that all nations that He has made shall come and worship before Him (Psalm 86:9; Acts 17:26). Indeed, the kingdom is the Lord and He rules over the nations (Psalm 22:28), and this includes the communities of the believers and the non-believers.

Although the Kingdom of God is not of this world, it is the supreme governing authority in this world. The world is not trees, hills, streams, or land, but it is humankind organizing its life apart from God (Psalm 2; 1 John 2:15-17; 4:4). The world as a moral factor represents the governments, institutions, organizations, laws, values, wisdom, knowledge, and lifestyles of fallen humanity seeking to discard the government of God. To say that the Kingdom of God is not of this world is to indicate its exclusion from the restraints or dictates of this world. The Kingdom of God is not defined by politics, economics, sociology, science, or any ideology. It is neither democratic, republican, conservative, nor liberal. In fact, the Kingdom of God is not restricted to religion. However, this does not mean that the Kingdom of God is not concerned with these areas of human existence. The concept that human existence is divided into spheres of the sacred (religious) and secular (athletics, politics, science, economics, entertainment, etc.) with the Kingdom of God being restricted to the religious sphere is erroneous. The Kingdom of God is not restricted to religious matters but encompasses all of creation; its principles and power are expressed in politics, science, economics, entertainment, athletics, and social welfare. Indeed, when the righteous rule, the people rejoice; but when the wicked man rules, the people groan (Prov. 29:2). Therefore, the prayer is "Lord, Let not an evil speaker be established in the earth" (Psalm 140:11).

CHAPTER 4

Expectation and The Realization of The Kingdom

The idea of the Kingdom of God is set forth in the Old Testament with its many symbols, types, and shadows. Even though there is the manifest expression of the sovereign rule of God in the Old Testament, the New Testament represents the realization of the much anticipated hopes and expectations (Luke 16:16; Gal. 3:22-26; 4:4-7; Heb. 1:1-4).

The sovereignty of God is expressed in the disclosure of truth. For example, it is not unusual for the Lord God to choose to say something earlier about a subject and not later; and to choose to reveal the subject to a select few and not to others (Gal. 4:1-5; Eph. 3:2-10; Heb. 1:1-2; 1 Pet. 1:9-12). This is referred to as the "scandal of peculiarity" and expresses the nature of a mystery in which a truth or a concept is hidden or partially understood and later revealed. It is the misunderstanding of this pattern of revealing truth that often creates a crisis between the anticipation and the realization of the idea of the Kingdom (2 Pet. 3:1-18).

Old Testament prophets are "Messianic predictors" while the New Testament apostles and prophets are "Messianic clarifiers." Peter writes that holy men of old speak as they are moved upon by the Holy Spirit (2 Pet.

1:20-21). However, these same messengers speak without a clear under-standing of their messages (1 Pet. 1:9-12). This understanding or clarifi-cation seems to be selectively given to apostles and prophets who succeed these Old Covenant messengers. Paul speaks of this selective understand-ing as being a "mystery" which in other ages is not made known to the sons of men as it is now revealed by the Spirit to His holy apostles and prophets (Eph. 3:3-12). In essence, what the Old Testament prophets foretell and predict to come without a clear understanding, the New Testament apostles and prophets give the meaning and the implication (Acts 2:14-36).

The Biblical idea of a mystery is something that is kept secret and then selectively disclosed at a particular time to a particular people. Hence, a mystery is a divine purpose that is hidden in the counsels of God that is finally revealed at an appointed time (1 Cor. 2:6-15) As aforementioned, this is referred to as the "scandal of peculiarity" in which God chooses to reveal something now and not later and to reveal it to this person and not to another.

Mark's gospel sets forth a group of parables that are the "mystery of the kingdom of God" (4:11). To understand this concept, it is necessary to view the future from an Old Testament perspective. For the citizens of the Old Covenant, the appearance of the Kingdom of God is anticipated as a single event in which the mighty manifestation of the power of God destroys the wicked kingdom of human rule and fills the earth with righ-teousness. In that day, God sets up His reign and displaces all other reigns, kingdoms, and authorities (Psalm 110:1, 5-7; Matt. 22:44; 1 Thes. 5:1-3; 2 Pet. 3:10). However, the parable of the tares demonstrates that wheat (the seeds of the Kingdom) and weeds (seeds of wickedness) co-exist until a time of harvest (Matt. 13:24-30; 38-39), but in the book of Daniel when the Kingdom comes, it destroys sinners and all wickedness from the earth (Dan. 2:34-45). Yet, this parable presents the co-existence of evil and righ-teousness. How can the Kingdom be actively here while the wicked and the righteous continue to live together in the world? The Kingdom is here in subtle power exercising its influence through persuasion. Its principles of righteousness are being demonstrated in the lives and communities of the redeemed. The confusion arrives when the Kingdom is viewed as an event rather than a process of transformation.

When Jesus casts out demons, He announces that the Kingdom is "at hand" and demonstrates that it is the manifestation of power and rule (Matt. 4:17; Luke 11:20). His teachings reveal how people may enter the Kingdom of God (Matt. 5:20; 7:21; John 3:5). However, His use of natural concepts to reveal spiritual realities presents a conflict in the minds of those who hear Him (John 3:3-12). For example, when Jesus stands before Pilate to be examined about His teachings, He states that His Kingdom is "not of this world" which indicates that the ethics, authority, structure, and foundation of the Kingdom have no comparison among the earthly political, economic, and social systems of the world (John 18:36). Such a statement can suggest that the Kingdom of God has nothing to do with the world. As aforementioned, if the world is understood to mean the earth, rather than the systems, institutions, organizations, and structures of human creation, then the Kingdom is thought to be purely a future, spiritual, and heavenly idea. However, when the world is understood to represent mankind with all of their devices and schemes seeking to govern themselves without God, then we understand the distinction between the Kingdom of the Lord Jesus and the ones that are constructed by humankind. Greed, avarice, competition, strife, contention, deceit, jealousy, covetousness, manipulation, wickedness, unfairness, and inequality characterize the "kingdoms of this world" (Matt. 4:8; Luke 4:5; Rev. 11:15). The Kingdom of God is righteousness, joy, and peace in the Holy Ghost (Rom. 14:17). So the parables of the Kingdom indicate that the Kingdom is present and at work in the world (Matt. 6: 10; 13:18-33; 37-52; Luke 13:18-21). Just like leaven transforms the entire loaf, so the Kingdom is "at hand" and working through the power of the Holy Spirit and the strategies of the redeemed community called the Church.

In His judgment of Israel, Jesus announces that the scribes and Pharisees close the door of the Kingdom to themselves and to others (Matt. 23:13) and hence the Kingdom is taken from them and given to a nation bearing the fruit of it (Matt. 21:43). The idea of the Kingdom being given to another nation is often misunderstood to represent the institutional Church (Matt. 16:18-19). However, Jesus qualifies the "nation" as being one that bears the fruit of the Kingdom. Although the "fruit" is not specifically stated, it can be assumed that it includes "righteousness, joy, and peace" (Rom. 2:17-24; 14:17). Such a misunderstanding of Matthew 21:43 can contribute to the belief that the Kingdom of God and the Church are synonymous. However, we shall see later that the Kingdom and the Church are indeed separate and distinct. Furthermore, grave suspicion arises when we consider the fruit of the contemporary institutional Church.

When the disciples inquire about the restoration of the Kingdom of God to Israel, Jesus directs their attention to the coming of the Holy Spirit and their responsibility for world evangelism (Matt. 24-25; Acts 1:6-8). In the Church community, the Holy Spirit is often understood to be a "Pentecostal phenomena" that is peculiar to a radical group of people who shout, dance, speak in tongues, and prophesy. To the contrary, the Holy Spirit is the norm of the Christian experience (Acts 2:38; 8:14-17; 9:17; 10:44-47) and inseparable from the Kingdom of God and evangelism (Rom. 14:17). While the Word is the intelligence of the Kingdom, the Holy Spirit is its power (Matt. 22:29). It is the Holy Spirit that serves as the Executive Agent of the Kingdom and the Mediator of all earthly activities related to its existence and power (Gen. 1:2; Joel 2:28; Zech. 4:6; Matt. 10:20; Luke 12:12; John 14:16, 16:7-14; Acts 1:2, 5, 8). Yet, when sections of the Church view the Holy Spirit as simply a doctrine or a "Pentecostal phenomena," then they attempt to influence society without understanding the power of the Kingdom. Then the Kingdom is viewed simply as implementing social actions such as feeding the poor, clothing the naked, and reforming the imprisoned. It is restricted to political and economic strategies of lobbying to change laws, legislation, and governments. Indeed, the Kingdom of God does involve government, laws, legislation, and social concerns, but the Kingdom is not restricted to human government, institutions, and organizations. Jesus says, "The Kingdom of God does not come with observation; nor will they say, 'See here!' or 'See there!' For the Kingdom of God is within you" (Luke 17:20-21). This is another way of saying that this "Pentecostal phenomena," called the Holy Spirit, is the essential dimension of the Kingdom.

The crisis between the anticipation and the realization of the Kingdom continues. The Rabbinical expectation concerning the Kingdom of God is taken from Old Testament references. There is the expectation of an age of plenty (Amos 9:13, 14; Isaiah 32:15, 35:1, 7; Jer. 31:12); an age of friendship (Hos. 2:18; Isaiah 11:6-9, 65:25); the end of pain (Isaiah 65:20, 22, 33:24); an age of peace (Isaiah 2:4, 11:9, 32:18); the supremacy of Israel (Isaiah 2:2, 3, 60:12; Mic. 4:1, 2); and the exaltation of Jerusalem (Isaiah 49:6; Zech. 14:17, 18). This view implies a national, ethnic, and geographic emphasis to the Kingdom of God. It indicates the extension of special privileges and responsibilities to a specific people, in a specific location, and at a specific time. This view declares that the Kingdom foretold by the prophets of old—especially when the prophecy relates to David or his house—is the earthly kingdom of Israel, and that the national restoration and earthly supremacy for the Jews is expected.

There exists a tension between the expectation of the Kingdom of God and the realization of the Kingdom of God in Jewish thought during the days of the Lord Jesus. When John the Baptist is cast into prison, he sends messengers to Jesus to ask if He is the Coming One, or should they look for another (Matt. 11:2-3). Why did John ask the question? Perhaps the Old Testament prophecies are not in the process of being fulfilled (Gen. 49:10). For example, Herod Antipas rules in Galilee. Legions of Roman armies patrol Jerusalem. Government and rule is in the hands of a pagan, Pilate of Rome, and Rome rules the world with a strong hand. The problem that faces John and every devout Jew is one of interpretation. How can Jesus be the bearer of the Kingdom while sin and evil institutions still remain unchanged? Jesus answers John's question indirectly and clarifies the problem (Matt. 11:4-6). Here is the mystery of the Kingdom in the way that it is presently working (Matt. 9:5-6, 8; Mark 6:7; 9:1; Luke 5:17-24, 31-32; 10:18-20; 11:20). It is yet to come in the form prophesied by Daniel and others, but it is also working now. Human rule and sin are now being abolished from the earth. The Kingdom is now here with persuasion and subtle power. Like the "soil" in the parable of Matthew 11, the mystery of the Kingdom is that it is here but not with irresistible power. It can be rejected (Matt. 23:13; Luke 7:29-35; 10:16).

It is predicted that "the scepter shall not depart from Judah, nor the ruler's staff from between his feet, until Shiloh comes. And to Him shall be the obedience of the people" (Gen. 49:10; Micah 5:2). According to this Scripture, two signs are to take place soon after the advent of the Messiah (Shiloh) and the Kingdom. The first sign is the removal of the scepter or identity of Judah. Judah is deprived of its national sovereignty during 70 years of the Babylonian captivity; however, it never loses its tribal staff or national identity during this time. They still possess their own lawgivers, or judges, while in captivity (Ezra 1:5, 8; Psalm 60:7; 108:8). The second sign is the suppression of judicial power through the restriction of the San-hedrin's legal power 23 years before the trial of Christ. The Bible notes the loss of the power to pass the death sentence (Matt. 27:1-2, 11-23; Mark

15:1214; Luke 23:1-11, 14-16, 21-25). All nations subdued by the Roman Empire are deprived of their ability to pronounce the capital sentence. The Romans take the legal power of the Sanhedrin from them, so they cover their heads with ashes and their bodies with sackcloth, exclaiming: "Woe unto us, for the scepter has departed from Judah, and the Messiah has not come." Little do they realize that their Messiah (Shiloh) is a young Nazarene walking in the midst of them, and neither do they understand that the "throne of God is forever and ever; a scepter of righteousness is the scepter of Your Kingdom" (Heb. 1:8). Shiloh has come and the power of rule is present also.

The Gospels give compelling evidence of how strong and alive is the idea of the Messiah and the Kingdom in the life of the people during the time of Jesus. However, the appearance and the ministry of Jesus do not correspond with Israel's hopes (Isaiah 9:5). For example, He exalts Himself above Abraham, Isaac, Jacob, and Moses (John 4:12); He declares Himself to be greater than the temple (Matt. 12:6); and He does not measure up to Israel's idea of a king (Isaiah 9:6; Luke 1:71, 74; Phil. 2:7). Jesus is a guest of sinners (Luke 15:1; 19:7); He pays taxes (Matt. 22:21), and He is homeless and without possessions (Luke 9:58). The Messiah is expected to come out of Bethlehem, and Jesus grows up in Nazareth and is a Galilean. Israel never considers a suffering Messiah and the idea that Jesus is conquered and crucified is too incredible to them (Luke 24:13-27; 1 Cor. 1:18-31). This crisis between the anticipation and the realization of the idea of the Messiah is one of the compelling reasons for the rejection and crucifixion of Jesus.

Our Lord Jesus makes many statements that indicate a transition is at hand with His coming. He speaks openly to a Samaritan woman and declares that "the hour is coming when you will neither on this mountain nor in Jerusalem, worship the Father;" for "the hour is coming, and now is, when the true worshipers will worship the Father in spirit and in truth" (John 4:21-23). He declares that the "Law and the Prophets were until John, but since that time the Kingdom of God is preached" (Luke 16:16). These statements and others are so often characterized with the phrase: "You have heard that it was said to those of old, but now I say unto you" (Matt. 5:21, 22, 27, 28, 33, 34). It is clear that something notable is changed, modified, or discontinued. What once serves as a standard of principle, practice, behavior, and belief is now supplanted by the coming of the Lord Jesus. For example, the blood of bulls, goats, and the sprinkling of a heifer no longer can purify (Heb. 9:19-28); a limited priesthood is changed to include a broader or universal priesthood (Heb. 7:12); a new and living way is made open to God (Heb. 10:20); the Holy Spirit is no longer selectively poured out but is poured out upon all flesh (Acts 2:16-21); government by kings, judges, and prophets, is now supplanted by a company of different ministers (Eph. 4:11-14); the delegation of privileges and rights based upon gender, race, socioeconomic status, and national origin is confronted (Gal. 6:15; Eph. 3:6; Col. 3:10-11), and the authority of evil and the power of death are overcome (1 Cor. 15:20-28; 50-57; Rev. 1:18). These are critical facts that affect the attitude and the behavior of the New Testament believers. If the believers continue to conduct themselves similar to the Galatians, who resort back to the law; the Hebrews, who refuse to progress and receive a better covenant; and the Colossians, who subject themselves to vain philosophies and traditions that are contrary to Christ, then they demonstrate their inability or unwillingness to accept and implement the privileges and responsibilities that are provided through the finished work of Christ and the present work of the Kingdom. They will continue to depend upon animal sacrifices, a temple made with hands, mediation through an earthly priesthood, and subjection to the fear of death and evil. They will continue to delegate earthly privileges and responsibilities based upon sex, race, socioeconomic status, and national origin. In order for New Testament believers to experience the privileges and the responsibilities that are not shared by Old Testament saints, these transitions must be understood and implemented.

The Lord Jesus also makes a further reference to the idea of the Kingdom in association with John the Baptist. He says that "from the days of John the Baptist until now the kingdom of heaven (Kingdom of God) suffers violence, and the violent take it by force" (Matt. 11:12). Could this statement have reference to some Rabbinical concepts and anticipated hopes regarding the Kingdom? Is it possible that what is realized and manifested in the life and ministry of Jesus presents a broader picture of the Kingdom than what is previously expected? Could the idea of the Kingdom transcend a single nation, a geographic location, and even a specific time? If this is so, then there emerges a crisis between the expectation and the realization of the Kingdom. Such a crisis does violence to the long held beliefs and anticipations of the coming Kingdom. This thought is substantiated by the fact that even the coming of the Lord Jesus is a "stumbling block" to the Jews and "foolishness" to the Greeks (1 Cor. 1:21-23). How much more the idea that the Kingdom is not to have headquarters in Jerusalem, exclusive of the Gentiles, and is to be headed by a king who prays for the enemies of Israel and does not bring the people into an expected time of peace, prosperity, and productivity. Indeed, the idea of the Kingdom suffers violence.

The implication of this conflict between anticipation and realization is described in terms that depict violence, war, division, and even death. The restricted view of the kingdom is now expanded to include citizens out of every kindred, tribe, tongue, and nations. Those who willingly enter into the implications of this expanded meaning of the kingdom are considered violent in the sense that they sacrifice family, friends, possessions, and even life itself for the sake of entering into its existence.

Is there any Biblical basis to substantiate the possibility that the prophets foretell such a concept of the kingdom? Well, the apostles use the language of the Old Testament to call attention to the close and vital connection that exists between the Old Testament Israel and the New Testament Church. Such language awakens the possibility that the burden of the Old Testament prophecy is not limited to one ethnic people but to all nations. It may be that through Israel and Israel's Messiah that the Gentiles are saved. All nations should "flow" to the mountain of the Lord's house. While the Old Testament infers, the New Testament makes clear the extent of the rights and privileges that the Gentiles enjoy through the acceptance of Israel's God. Could it be that these rights are so extensive that "the earthly distinction of Jew and Gentile" is diminished? If this proposition is so, is it "a wholly new thing" or is it something that is already foretold? A brief summary of apostolic preaching testifies to the proposition that the prophets foretell the vital connection between the Old Testament and the New Testament:

1. In Acts 1:8, the phrase "unto the uttermost part of the earth" occurs also in Isaiah 49:6, where Israel is given as a light to the Gentiles and for the salvation unto the end of the earth. The Great Commission has a global scope.

2. In Acts 2:16-40, Peter uses Old Testament references. He refers to Joel 2:29-32 to validate the outpouring of the Spirit as already predicted. At the end of the message, Peter makes an appeal to "all the house of

Israel" and to "whosoever will." Peter appeals to Psalms 110 to show that the Lord Jesus has already received and is now exercising His royal authority. Hence, the kingdom is now "come" and a redeemed people is now initiated into the fulfillment of the Messianic prophecy.

3. In Acts 3:12-26, Peter refers three times to the testimony of "the prophets" and also to Moses and to the Abrahamic covenant, saying that "Yea and all the prophets from Samuel and them that followed after, as many as have spoken, they also told of these days."

4. In Acts 7:48, the statement that "Howbeit the Most High dwelleth not in temples made with hands," is supported by an appeal to Isaiah 66:1-2, which can indicate that an earthly temple no longer has a legitimate place. Stephen applies Isaiah's words to the Church, when he says that "Heaven is my throne, and the earth is my footstool, where is the house that ye built me, and where is the place of my rest? For all these things hath mine hand made."

5. In Acts 8:26-40, Phillip's preaching to the Ethiopian eunuch and his conversion is brought about through applying Isaiah 53 to those events which the Church is founded.

6. In Acts 10, which records the conversion of Cornelius and his household, Peter concludes the gospel with a direct appeal to prophecy: "To him bear all the prophets witness, that through his name everyone that believeth on him shall receive remission of sins" (v. 43). It is obvious that "everyone" includes Jews and Gentiles.

7. In Acts 13:40-41, Paul includes many quotes from Psalms 2, 16, Isaiah 55, and Habakkuk 1:5 in his discourse in the synagogue at Pisidian Antioch. Both Paul and Barnabas justify their ministry to the Gentiles through Isaiah 49:6, "I will give thee for a light to the Gentiles, that thou mayest be my salvation unto the end of the earth."

8. In Acts 15:13, the testimonies of Peter and Paul before the Council at Jerusalem concerning the nature of the Church and the relationship between the Jew and Gentile, James summarizes the testimonies by an appeal to the prophets: "And to this agree the words of the prophets; as it is written, after these things I will return, and I will build the

tabernacle of David, which is fallen, and I will build again the ruins thereof, and I will set it up; that the residue of men may seek after the Lord, and all the Gentiles, upon whom my name is called, said the Lord, who maketh these things known from of old" (Amos 9:11). The phrase, "I will build again" refers to the first advent and to the redemptive work, which will culminate in the Second Advent. It is a reference to the Church and the salvation of the Gentiles. It is alleged that the phrase, "I will raise up the tabernacle of David which is fallen" has reference to a future Davidic kingdom; however, the thought must be entertained that one greater than David, Jesus the Lord, rose triumphant over death and commissioned His disciples with His own claim of sovereignty.

9. In Acts 24:14, Paul's defense before Felix, is affirmed with the testimony that Paul himself believes all things which are according to the law, and which are written in the prophets. Paul makes no reference to the Church as an interruption or a parenthesis.

10. In Acts 26:6, 22, 27, Paul opens his defense before Agrippa with the words, "for the hope of the promise made of God unto our father" (vv. 6), in which he refers to the Abrahamic covenant. Paul claims that since his conversion, he has spoken nothing that is "outside of," "beyond," or "in addition to" what the prophets and Moses did say should come, that the death and resurrection of Christ, will be a source of light to "the people" (Jews) and to the nations (Gentiles) (Isaiah 49:6; Luke 2:32).

11. In Acts 28:20, Paul claims that "For the hope of Israel I am bound with this chain." In Galatians 6:16, Paul makes it very clear that the hope of the world is also the hope Jew and Gentile alike.

12. In Hebrews 8:8-12, there is very clear evidence to show how the Old Testament types are fulfilled in the New Testament realities. The reference to Jeremiah 31:31-34 is a clear indication that the new covenant rests upon the sacrifice of Christ, and secures the eternal blessings under the Abrahamic Covenant (Gal. 3:13-20) for all who will believe.

13. In Romans 9:25-26, Paul refers to Hosea 2:23 as a record of Israel dis-obedience and God's response. Although the prophecy might literally

refer to Israel, Paul sees that the phrase "Not my people," may mean either "no longer my people" or "not yet my people." Paul believes that the fulfillment of this prophecy refers to the Jews and to the Gentiles respectively. For Paul, Hosea foretells the calling of "vessels of mercy… not from the Jews only, but also from the Gentiles."

14. In 2 Corinthians 6:2, Paul makes a strong appeal to Isaiah 49:8 and declares that "now" is the "accepted time" and that "now" is the "day of salvation."

These summaries testify to the reality of the connection between the Old Testament and the New Testament and they also bear witness to the "violence" that erupts whenever such parallels are mentioned by the apostles.

It is clear that God uses a particular nation and race to reveal Himself to the world. Israel is chosen for a fourfold mission: (1) to witness to the revelation of God in the midst of universal idolatry; (2) to demonstrate the benefits of covenant obedience to Jehovah God; (3) to receive, preserve, and transmit the Scriptures; and (4) to produce as to His humanity, the Lord Jesus Christ. Indeed, the covenant with Israel is clearly stated: "Now, therefore, if ye will obey My voice indeed, and keep My covenant, then ye shall be a peculiar treasure unto Me above all people, for all the earth is mine" (Exodus 19:5). Even so, are the events of the Old Testament "ensamples," or types, that prefigure things to come (1 Cor. 10:11)? Could there be a New Testament connection or a fulfillment that is associated with the terms "nations of priest," a "peculiar people," and the "Israel of God" which appear in the Old Testament? This reality is shown since "the crisis of prophecy" is always the violent departure that the realized fulfillment assumes in reference to the expected fulfillment.

CHAPTER 5

Crisis After Pentecost

After Pentecost, the apostles and disciples speak openly of the Kingdom (Acts 8:12; 14:22; 19:8; 20:25; 28:23, 31; Rom. 14:17; 1 Cor. 4:20; 2 Thess. 1:3-5). The evangelistic campaign of Philip in Samaria is accompanied with miracles, and there is great success when the people believed his preaching "the things concerning the kingdom of God and the name of Jesus Christ" (Acts 8:5-12). Paul declares that the Kingdom is "not in word but in power" (1 Cor. 4:20) and that it is "righteousness and peace and joy in the Holy Spirit" (Rom. 14:17). Each of these two references by Paul suggests a connection between the Kingdom of God and the person of the Holy Spirit. Since the Holy Spirit is poured out upon all flesh (Joel 2:28-29; Acts 2:38-39), the idea of the Kingdom of God in its association with the Holy Spirit encompasses a broader audience of people, nations, and tongues (Rev. 5:9).

After Pentecost, the messengers who proclaim the principles of the Kingdom and demonstrate the dimensions of its power are referred to as ambassadors who plead and persuade people to be reconciled to God (2 Cor. 5:11, 20; 13:3-4; Heb.6:1-6). They are scorned and rejected (1 Cor. 4:9-13). The message of the Cross and the fact that the Kingdom comes not with the construction of political or social organizations may account for the criticisms of the apostles (1 Cor. 1:21-25; 2 Pet. 3:1-15). Peter refers to "scoffers" who mock the preaching of the apostles because the evidence of the Kingdom is not according to the expectation of the people (2 Pet. 3:3). For them, there is no change and Christ is not yet come. Like others before them, they neglect the significance of the First Coming of Jesus Christ and misunderstand the power of the Holy Spirit (1 Thes. 5:1-ll; 2 Thes. 2:1-12).

With the passing of time, what comes to be known as Pentecostalism emphasizes that the baptism in the Holy Spirit and the supernatural enablement to witness for Jesus Christ is an integral part of the plan of God.[2] The Spirit binds the redeemed community together with the coming of the Kingdom of God in the future. Because the Second Coming of Jesus is the central concern of the initial Pentecostal message, this group as a rule, do not visualize the social and cosmic dimensions of God's plan and tend to narrow the focus to the individual. Interesting enough, the theme to express the focus of the Pentecostal message in found in Matthew 24:14, which is to preach the Gospel to the world as a last call of the Lord and to sound the midnight cry.[3]

Many Pentecostals are fascinated with the rule of God through the Spirit and neglect the rule of God through creation and providence. This results in an emphasis on individual spirituality so that the reality of the Spirit is merely experienced in the experience.[4] The Kingdom is the rule of God and God rules in the Spirit. But does the Kingdom come only by the working of the Spirit though and within the redeemed community and exclude socio-political organizations and structures? When the Kingdom comes, will it bring all things under subjection to Christ including the political, intellectual, and the private spheres of life? Paul states that God's

---

2   See Howard M. Ervin, *Spirit Baptism: A Biblical Investigation* (Peabody, Mass.: Hendrickson Publishers, 1987); and James D.G. Dunn, *Baptism in the Holy Spirit* (Philadelphia: Westminster Press, 1970).

3   D. William Faupel, *The Everlasting Gospel: The Significance of Eschatology in the Development of Pentecostal Thought* (Sheffield, England: Sheffield Academic Press, 1996), p. 21.

4   Gordon Fee, *Paul, the Spirit, and the People of God* (Peabody, Mass.: Hendrickson Publishers, 1996), p. xiv.

plan is not simply to save individual souls, but also to fill all things with Himself so that, at the end, He will be all in all (Col. 1:19).

In contrast to the Pentecostals, the idea of a Christocracy presents the Kingdom of God as the model for the social, political, and economic organization of society. It is the belief that God rules through the social, political, and economic spheres. We will see that advocates of this concept visualize the rule of God through Christian political leaders of structures. The reign of God includes the individual and the cosmos. The Church is perceived as the custodian of society and the representative of God's rule on earth.

Among the historic and the contemporary Church, there develops factions of thought regarding the concept of the Kingdom. For example, William Barclay defines the Kingdom as the sovereignty, lordship, rule and reign of God.[5] Herman Ridderbos sees in the Old Testament a general and a particular kingship of the Lord.[6] The former (general) concerns the universal power and dominion of God over the whole world and all the nations, and is founded in the creation of heaven and earth (Ex. 15:18; 1 Kings 22:19; Isaiah 6:5; Psalm 47:3; 103:19). The latter (particular) denotes the special relation between the Lord and Israel (Num. 23:21; Judges 8:23; 1 Sam. 8:7; 12:12; Psalm 48:3; Isaiah 41:21; Jer. 8:19; Micah 2:13). This is called a theocracy and coincides with God's covenant in the Old Testament.

Adolf von Harnack presents the Kingdom of God in terms of the human spirit and its relationship with God. The Kingdom of God is an inward power, which enters into the human soul and lays hold of it. It consists of some basic religious truths that have universal application.[7] Georgia Harkness in her book, Understanding the Kingdom of God, writes that the entrance into the Kingdom is "through the Holy Spirit wisdom, strength, and guidance for living; comfort in sorrow; hope in adversity; outreach

---

5   William Barclay, *The King and the Kingdom* (Grand Rapids, Mich.: Baker Book House, 1980), 98.

6   Herman Riddderbos, *The Coming of the Kingdom* (Philadelphia, Pa.: The Presbyterian and Reformed Publishing Co., 1962), 4.

7   A. Harnack, *What Is Christianity?* (New York: Putnam's, 1901. E.T. of Das Wesen Christentums, Leipzig: Hinrich, 1900).

in service to others; and an abiding sense of the forgiving and sustaining presence of God."[8]

Charles Colson in his book, "Kingdom in Conflict," expresses the view of the Kingdom as being spiritual but not irrelevant to this world. In Colson's concept, the Kingdom of God is both present and future with its present form being unseen and spiritual. Yet, the Kingdom of God influences every aspect of life. He sees the Kingdom as not simply an outline for a new social order or simply a catalyst for some radical cultural change. The Kingdom of God demands a transformation of people in order to change society.[9]

Albrecht Ritschl (1822-1889) gives a definition of the Kingdom of God as consisting of those who exercise righteousness and treat one another with love without regard to differences of sex, rank, or race, thereby bringing about a fellowship of moral attitude and moral properties extending through the whole range of human life. He believes that through the exercise of righteousness, the Kingdom of God is come into being within a short space in the community of the followers of Christ, in a manner that is exemplified by the growth of the seed and the working of leaven in dough.[10]

C.H. Dodd in his book, The Parables of the Kingdom, interprets the parables and sayings of Jesus to mean that the Kingdom is come."[11] He conceives of the Kingdom as not future but it is a present fact, which men must recognize, accept or reject, by their actions. It is the absolute, the "wholly other" which is entered into time and space in the person of Jesus of Nazareth.

At the other end of the spectrum is Albert Schweitzer who defines Jesus' message of the Kingdom as an apocalyptic realm to be inaugurated by a

---

8   Georgia Harkness, *Understanding the Kingdom of God* (Nashville: Abingdon Press, 1974), p. 142.

9   Charles Colson with Ellen Santilli Vaughn, *Kingdoms in Conflict* (New York: William Morrow and Zondervan Publishing House, 1987), p. 86.

10   Albrecht Ritschl, *Rechtfertigung and Versohnung*, vol. ii. p. 31, Quoted in Gosta Lundstrom, *The Kingdom of God in the Teaching of Jesus* (Richmond: John Know Press, 1963), p.5.

11   CH. Dodd, *The Parables of the Kingdom* (London: Nisbet, 1935).

supernatural act of God when history will end and a new heavenly order of existence begins. The Kingdom of God is not seen as a present or a spiritual reality but it is future and supernatural.[12]

Other post-Pentecostal interpretations relate the Kingdom of God to the institutional Church (Matt. 16:18-19). This view is popularized since the days of Augustine's City of God (354-430), in which he speaks of the Church as God's present kingdom and even says that even now the saints reign with Him.[13] In this view, God reigns now on earth through the institutional Church and its structures of authority. The visible Church is the symbol and representative of the invisible reign of God over all creation. The Church building is "God's house," and the people are the royal priesthood of God. Consequently, as the Church grows, the Kingdom grows and is extended into the world. As the Church takes the Gospel into the entire world, it extends the Kingdom of God. Hence, the Church work and the Kingdom work are viewed as being synonymous.

L. Berkhof notes that the Reformers identify the Kingdom of God with the invisible Church, the community of the elect, or the saints of God. The reign of God in the heart of the believers does not neglect the existence of delegated authority in civil government. However, the Reformers do not expect the external visible form of the Kingdom of God to appear before the Second Coming.[14]

E. Stanley Jones, a Methodist missionary (1884-1973), sees the Kingdom of God in a theological and practical framework that is useful for the transformation of the individual and society. In his book, Christ's Alternative to Communism, Jones sets forth the demand for the application of the gospel of the Kingdom in society.[15] He visualizes the Kingdom as a force that works within, and not without, by moral persuasion and not by force. It is a radical change capable of bringing about human equality and the

---

12   Albert Schweitzer, *The Mystery of the Kingdom of God* (London: Black, 925).

13   Augustine, *The City of God*, trans. Marcus Dods (New York: The Modern Library, 1950).

14   L. Berkhof, *The Kingdom of God: The Development of the Idea of the Kingdom, Especially Since the Eighteenth Century* (Grand Rapids: Eerdmans, 1951), p. 24.

15   E. Stanley Jones, *Christ's Alternative to Communism* (Nashville: Abingdon Press, 1968), p. 148-49.

sharing of rights and privileges on an equal basis. For Jones, the Kingdom is both material and spiritual, both inward and outward, and capable of transforming the world.[16] He insists that the Church and the Kingdom are not identical. The Kingdom is divine action and design but also involves human participation. He writes:

Christ loved the Church and gave Himself for it that He might redeem it. But He never gives Himself for the Kingdom to redeem it. For the Kingdom is itself redemption. It is not the subject of redemption—it offers it. The difference is profound. The Church may be, and is, the agent of the coming of that redemption, but it is the agent and not the absolute. I am bound to be loyal to the Church to the degree that it is loyal to the Kingdom, but my highest loyalty is to the Kingdom, and when these loyalties conflict, then I must bow the knee finally to the Kingdom. Any false loyalty to the Church, which would make it take the place of the Kingdom, is destructive to the Church.[17]

Luther in his "two kingdoms" and Calvin in his "Genevan theocracy'" seem to project a political concept of divine authority. However, Luther visualizes the Kingdom as an inward spiritual experience. He looks forward to the future kingdom in its fullness when all creation will be reconciled after the destruction of the world by fire.[18] Because both Luther and Calvin are convinced that all authority comes from God, they project the belief that leaders exercise governmental stewardship according to Biblical truth. It is Luther's view that the state is God's delegated authority to restrain evil and confusion and to promote the righteousness of God. Hence, the state is a divine institution to promote the cause of God. He writes the following:

There are two kingdoms, one the kingdom of God, the other the kingdom of the world... God's kingdom is a kingdom of grace and mercy... but the kingdom of the world is a kingdom of wrath and severity... Now he who

---

16   E. Stanley Jones, *The Unshakeable Kingdom and the Unchanging Person* (Nashville: Abingdon Press, 1940).

17   E. Stanley Jones, *Is The Kingdom of God Realism?* (New York: Abingdon Press, 1940), p. 58-59.

18   Martin Luther, *The Bondage of the Will*, quoted in Paul Althaus, *The Theology of Martin Luther*, trans. Robert C. Schultz (Philadelphia: Fortress Press, 1966), p. 163.

would confuse these two kingdoms -as our false fanatics do - would put wrath into God's kingdom and mercy into the world's kingdom; and that is the same as putting the devil in heaven and God in hell.[19]

Calvin envisions political leaders making laws in agreement with Biblical principles. His concept of separation of Church and state does not agree with our contemporary understanding of this concept. For Calvin, the Church and the state are to co-exist, serving and ruling the same people with mutual respect and support. The Church is not to prescribe civil laws and the state is not to supplant spiritual discipline. However, the Church reserves the right to speak to the state.[20]

A Calvinist pastor by the name of Abraham Kuyper (1837-1920) spearheads in a lifetime a comprehensive movement that addresses every facet of national life with a coherent theology and a specific program.[21] Under his leadership, Christians control the largest newspaper in the nation; begin the Free University in Amsterdam to educate in terms of their perspective; establish a national Christian day school movement; initiate a new Christian denomination; develop a political party, which controls the legislature for over a decade; and form a Christian labor union. This movement is credited with the development of modern European civilization and its finest fruits; progressive science and emancipated art; and constitutional republican movement and civil liberties.

Christian Reconstructionism, Dominion Theology, and Theonomy are interrelated beliefs.[22] Christian Reconstructionism is a belief that society, particularly in the United States, is seriously degenerated morally and religiously and must be totally rebuilt to Biblical standards. This concept is based on the belief that through the establishment and enforcement of Old Testament civil law that America can become reconciled to God. The

---

19   Heinrich Bomkamm, *Luther's Word of Thought*, trans. Martin H. Bertram (St. Louis: Concordia Publishing House, 1965), p.245.

20   John Calvin, Sermon on 1 Samuel 42. Quoted in W. Fred Braham, *The Constructive Revolutionary: John Calvin and His Socio-Economic Impact* (Richmond: John Knox Press, 1971), p. 158-59.

21   James D. Bratt, *Dutch Calvinism in Modern America: A History of a Conservative Subculture* (Grand Rapids: Wm. B. Eerdmans Publishing Co., 1984), p. 14.

22   Ibid. p. 16.

Christian mandate, according to the Reconstruction view, is both soul-winning and culture-winning. It provides for a thriving agriculture, commerce, industry, and a purified family life. The promotion of these concepts is attributed much to the efforts of Rousas A.J. Rushdoony, Greg Bahnsen, and Gary North.[23]

Dominion Theology is derived from Genesis 1:26 of the Hebrew Scriptures:

Then God said, "Let us make man in our image, in our likeness and let them rule over the fish of the sea and the birds of the air, over the livestock, over all the earth and over all the creatures that move along the ground."

The interpretation of this verse is used to support the concept that God gives mankind dominion over the kingdoms of this world. Hence, Dominion theologians believe that this verse commands Christians to bring societies, around the world, under the rule of the Word of God. The Great Commission to the Church, according to this view, does not end simply with witnessing to the nations. The kingdoms of the world are to become the kingdoms of Christ. The nations are to be trained and made obedient to the faith. This view advocates that the salvation of the individual and also the transformation of the surrounding environment of government, commerce, and social welfare can be accomplished through the same principles of redemption.[24]

Theonomy is the concept that all of the non-ceremonial laws given to Moses and recorded in the Pentateuch are binding for people of all nations forever. The extreme methodology of such a belief system advocates a peaceful conversion of the United States government to a theocracy that is based on the Mosaic Law. These principles are to be used to train a generation of children in private Christian religious schools. Upon their gradu-

---

23 A summary of books by these authors include Rushdoony's *Institute of Biblical Law* (Philadelphia, N.J.: Presbyterian & Reformed Publishing Co., 1973); Gary North's *Dominion and Common Grace: The Biblical Basis of Progress* (Tyler, Tex.; Institute fro Christian economics, 1987); and Greg Bahnsen's *Theonomy in Christian Ethics* (Phillipsburg, N.J.; Presbyterian & Reformed Publishing Co., 1977).

24 David Chilton, *Paradise Restored: An Eschatology of Dominion* (Tyler, Tex.: Reconstruction Press, 1985).

ation they are to be charged with the responsibility of creating a Biblically based economic, political, religious, and social order. Religious freedom is eliminated and the entire world is converted to Christianity. All religions other than Christianity are suppressed. Society is administered according to the Hebrew Scriptures. All idolatry and contrary religious beliefs are exterminated.[25]

The idea of Puritanism has a commitment to establishing a Christian society in America. The Puritans desire a government that is confirmed rigidly to the civil codes of the Old Testament, thereby creating a model of the Kingdom of God on earth.[26]

The proclamation and the demonstration of the Church are significant in the economy of the Kingdom.[27] The Gospel must not only offer individual salvation to believers, but it must also set forth the purpose and strategies necessary to transform all the relationships of life here and now and thus cause the Kingdom of God to prevail in all the world. The Gospel has the power to transform the social, economic, and political systems while it authorizes the spiritual regeneration of the individual believers. The Kingdom of God is like leaven that slowly transforms the world by a gradual influence.

Still, other post-Pentecostal thinkers present the Kingdom of God as an ideal pattern for human society. According to this concept, the Kingdom is not totally concerned with individual salvation or with the future but with the present social order and its problems. Here the Kingdom of God is established as people work for the ideal social order and offer solutions to the problems of poverty, sickness, social inequities, and race relationshiPsalm.[28] This view may be the basic motivation behind the efforts of

---

25 Greg Bahnsen, *Theonomy in Christian Ethics* (Phillipsburg, N.J.: Presbyterian & Reformed Publishing Co., 1977).

26 Lelan Ryken, *Worldly Saints: The Puritans as They Really Were* (Grand Rapids, Mich.: Academic Books, Zondervan Publishing House, 1986).

27 Earl Paulk and Dan Rhodes, *A Theology for the New Millennium* (Atlanta, Ga.: Earl Paulk Ministries, 2000).

28 Walter Rauschenbusch, *The Righteousness of the Kingdom* (Nashville and New York: Abingdon Press, 1968). See also *Christianity and the Social Crisis* (1907) and *A Theology for the Social Gospel* (1917).

religious groups to form monastic communities and "perfect societies." It may also serve as the foundation of liberation theologies that advocate the formation of new societies of justice and equality. This view perceives evil to be environmental and neglects the depravity of sin and its dominion over unbelieving people.

Considering such diversity of post-Pentecostal interpretations of the Kingdom, is there a single opinion that is promoted in the Scriptures? It appears that the Scriptures offer a diversity of statements about the Kingdom of God. For example, the Kingdom of God is a present reality (Matt. 12:28; 21:31; Rom. 14:17) and a future blessing (1 Cor. 15:50; 2 Pet. 1:11; Matt. 8:11). It is an inner spiritual blessing (Rom. 14:17), which is experienced only by way of the new birth (John 3:3), and yet it will involve the government of the nations of the world (Rev. 11). It is a gift of God to be given in the future (Luke 12:32), and yet it is received in the present (Mark 10:15). It is an inheritance that God will bestow upon His people when Christ comes again (Matt. 25:34), and yet it is also a realm that believers enter now (Col. 1:13).

The issue of the "present but not yet" dimension of the Kingdom of God is most interesting (Mark 1:15; Matt. 6:10). The early Church experiences the "already" dimension of the Kingdom in the person and ministry of Jesus and in the coming of the Holy Spirit after Pentecost. They also experience the "not yet" dimension in the promise of the Second Coming of Jesus and in the Lord's own words about the end times (Matt. 24). However, the burden of apostolic preaching in the book of Acts and the epistles does not focus upon future events. In the Pauline epistles, the "new creation" is already present (2 Cor. 5:17). Believers are already delivered from the power of darkness and "translated into the Kingdom of His dear Son" (Col. 1:13). The rebirth of the believer is a present reality (1 Pet. 1:3, 23), and they currently taste "the powers of the Age to come" (Heb. 6:6). The crisis of history is a past event and not simply an anticipated future occurrence. The critical attention of apostolic preaching is that God visits and redeems His people as demonstrated in the birth, ministry, crucifixion, resurrection, ascension of Christ, and the pouring out of the Holy Spirit. Hence, apostolic preaching makes reference to the Second Coming of Christ but stakes its claims on the fact that Christ is come (Acts 3:20-21, 10:42).

The good news of the Gospel is that Jesus Christ is the "power of God unto salvation," and that faith in His finished work on Calvary is the hope of the nations (Rom. 1:16). The Second Coming of the Lord is the damnation of any who do not accept the Gospel (Matt. 24:14; 25:1-13; Luke 1:76-79; 2 Cor. 6:2).

Despite any national, ethnic, or geographic associations, it is clear that the Kingdom of God provides the occasion for a variety of opinions. All factions agree on its existence but disagree on its implications. Nevertheless, the Kingdom is the government of God and therefore the vehicle of all divine revelation. It is based upon the incarnation, life, ministry, death and resurrection of the Son of David (Acts 10:38); which is introduced with power by the coming of the Holy Spirit (1 Tim. 3:16); and which is extended throughout all the nations of earth, and through all the centuries of this era of grace (Acts 10:34-36, 42-31) "by those who have preached the gospel with the Holy Ghost sent down from above" (1 Pet. 1:12). The Son of David saves sinners from among all nations and rebuilds the House of God (Acts 15:15-17). The Son of David suffers and dies before He reigns, whether in heaven or on earth (Acts 2:34-36; 1 Cor. 15:24-28; Heb. 1:13; 10:12). Hence, the proclamation of the Kingdom is the revelation of God's intention in creation and His will in heaven being done on earth. The revelation of this will is founded upon the death and the resurrection of the "Son," the "Christ of God," who also is God's "King," spoken of by David in the Second Psalm.

The Kingdom of God and A Worldview

In the New Testament, the term "world" or "cosmos" refers to the order of society and indicates that evil has a social and a political character. The most distinctive aspect of this concept of the "world" in the New Testament is a system of values that are in opposition to God. Consequently, the world is viewed as the evil social order with all of its schemes and institutions seeking to govern itself in opposition to God (Luke 4:5; John 17:11, 15, 16; 18:36; Eph. 2:1-2; 1 John 2:15-17). It includes economic relationships (1 Cor. 7:31); a system of wisdom and knowledge (1 Cor. 1:20; Matt. 4:88); and even property and wealth (1 John 3:17). Hence, the idea of the world is not a place but a collective organization of councils, plans, government, ideology, wisdom, knowledge, and systems of human relationships that seek to silence the representative voice of God in the earth. The world is a moral concept of human construction, whereas the earth is the Lord's with all of its lands, trees, rivers, mountains, and valleys.

First of all, a worldview is the frame of reference we use to evaluate life. A worldview includes the assumptions and convictions that tell us what is true and valuable and what is not, and it helps interpret what is right or wrong and serves as the basis of daily decisions. James Sire writes more specifically that a worldview is "a set of presuppositions (or assumptions) which we hold (consciously or unconsciously) about the basic makeup of our world."[29] According to Sire, "a worldview is composed of a number of basic presuppositions, more or less self-consistent, generally unquestioned by each person, rarely, if ever, mentioned to one's friends, and only brought to mind when challenged by a foreigner from another ideological universe."[30]

A worldview will answer five basic questions according to Sire:

1. What is really real?

2. What does it mean to be human?

3. What happens to us at death?

4. What is the basis of morality?

5. What is the meaning of history?

These questions are not totally inclusive. There are other issues that arise such as, "Who is in charge of the world? Is it God, or man, the devil, or no one at all?"

According to Sire, everyone assumes some answers to these questions. We adopt either one stance or another. Refusing to adopt an explicit worldview turns out to be itself a worldview or at least a philosophic position. In short, we are caught. So long as we live, "we will live either the examined or the unexamined life."[31]

Danah Zohar refers to a worldview as a "theme running through a life," bringing everything together "into a coherent whole." A worldview "finds answers to life's 'big questions' such as: who am I, why am I here, and what is my place in the scheme of things, why is the world like it is, what

---

29 James W. Sire, *The Universe Next Door: A Basic Worldview Catalog* (Downers Grove, 111.; Inter Varsity Press, 1976), 17-18.

30 Ibid. 18-19.

31 Ibid. 18-19.

it means that one day I must die?" According to Zohar, a comprehensive worldview encompasses the personal, social, and spiritual dimensions of life. "A successful worldview must, in the end, draw all these levels—the personal, the social, and the spiritual—into one coherent whole. If it does so, the individual has access to some sense of who he is, why he is here, how he relates to others, and how it is valuable to behave. If it does not, the world it was meant to articulate will fragment and the individual will suffer alienation on some level, perhaps on all levels."[32]

Phillips and Brown project a worldview as an explanation and an interpretation of the world and the application of such a view.[33] In basic terms, a worldview is a view *of the* world and a *view for* the world.

A productive worldview answers the critical questions of purpose, design, relationship, and the future. Why are we here? Where are we going? Who is in charge? Can we change things? Is there hope in the future? And how do we relate to other people? The answers to these questions reveal a perspective of the Kingdom of God since they address the three basic concerns: (1) the intervention of God in human affairs; (2) the revelation and restoration of divine purposes and intentions; and (3) human response to such divine knowledge. So let us examine two worldviews as they relate to these three basic concerns:

> **Theism**. This is the view that God is sovereign and the ultimate creator, organizer, and maintainer of all being, both material and immaterial. Theism assumes many different forms but its central theme is that God exists; creates all things; and interacts with His creation. This is the fundamental view held by Judaism, Christianity, and Islam.[34]

---

32 Danah Zohar, *The Quantum Self: Human Nature and Consciousness Defined by the New Physics* (New York: William Morrow, 1990), 232-33.

33 W. Gary Phillips and William E. Brown, *Making Sense of Your World*, (Chicago, Il.: Moody Press, 1991), 29.

34 F.L. Cross and E.A. Livingstone, *The Oxford Dictionary of the Christian Church*, (Oxford University Press 1974).

Deism. This view holds that the universe is created by God with design, order, and purpose. Yet God is not involved with the ongoing life of this world. Deism presents God as being remote, passive, and maybe irrelevant. The fundamental view is that the universe derives its order and purpose from divine action and intention.[35]

The difference between these two worldviews lies in the nature of God and the degree of God's involvement in the ongoing activity of the world. Deism presents God as creator who exerts no ongoing influence on people or the world. Conversely, theism presents God as creator and as being personal and continually involved in the affairs of the universe.

The writings of the prophets clearly indicate that God is personal, moral, and involved with the affairs of this life. Note the prophet Isaiah's description of the sovereignty of God Who is involved with His people:

> *Hast thou not known? Has thou not heard, that the everlasting God the Lord, the Creator of the ends of the earth, fainteth not, neither is weary? There is no searching of his understanding. He giveth power to the faint; and to them that have no might he increaseth strength. Even the youths shall faint and be weary, and the young men shall utterly fall; But they that wait upon the Lord shall renew their strength.* (Isaiah 40:28-31)

> *Is not this the fast that I have chosen? To loose the bands of wickedness, to undo the heavy burden, and to let the oppressed go free, and that ye break every yoke? Is it not to deal thy bread to the hungry, and that thou bring the poor that are cast out to thy house? When thou seest the naked that thou cover him; and that thou hide not thyself from thine own flesh? Then shall thy light break forth as the morning, and thine health shall spring forth speedily.* (Isaiah 58:6-8)

---

35   Ibid.

These prophetic expressions reveal a God of justice, compassion, and mercy and One who is involved with the affairs of human life. Even the heathen king Nebuchadnezzar, after his exile to dwell with the beasts of the field, openly declares that "the most high ruleth in the kingdom of men and giveth it to whomsoever he will" and "whose dominion is an everlasting dominion, and his kingdom is from generation to generation" (Dan. 4:1-34).

In the theistic worldview, God is moral, just, and makes moral and ethical demands upon His subjects (Psalm 21:3; 89:14; 103:6; 146:7; Amos 5:21-24; Micah 6:6-8). Ultimately it is the Lord Jesus Christ who presents the Father as One who "desires mercy and not sacrifice" (Matt. 12:7). The theistic worldview defines the meaning of such terms as "judge," "transform," "leaven," and "occupy" (1 Cor. 6:2; Rom. 12:2; Luke 19:13; Matt. 13:33; Mark 8:15). Such terms are set forth in the Scriptures to define the relationship that God establishes between the redeemed community and the world (Matt. 28:18-20; Mark 16:15-18; Luke 13:21, 19:13; Rom. 12:1-2; Gal. 5:9). The Lord Jesus never prays for the disciples to be taken out of the world but that they may be delivered from the evil (John 17:6-22). There is a sense in which the disciples become "cultural architects," and not "cultural critics," who are empowered with the knowledge and authority to facilitate a transformation of their world. Even the Great Commission "to make disciples of all the nations" is a command to be active and not passive.

Let us explore the position of a theistic worldview and how this relates to the concept of the Kingdom of God, the Church, and the world.

It is interesting that whenever there are widespread revivals and spiritual awakenings in a society, there are also times of social reforms. Revival movements are supposed to awaken the spiritual and ethical consciousness of a society. Since people are the vehicles of God's righteousness, evangelism should contribute to the moral changes in people. It is difficult to build an expanding foundation of social and political righteousness upon a decreasing foundation of faith in God that comes through evangelism. Therefore, the strategies of evangelism should not be restricted to individual conversions and exclude the cultural, social, economical, and political concerns of a society.

The Evangelical Revival is the initiator and nurturer of a new social conscious and a passion for social justice. The Evangelical Revival transforms the moral character of the general populace more than any movement in British history. The reason for such an impact is the strategy of preaching the gospel, converting sinners to Christ, and inspiring people to assume social causes in the name of Christ. Historians attribute John Wesley's influence rather than any other to the fact that Britain is spared the horrors of a bloody revolution like France's. This premise is explored by J. Wesley Bready in his book *England Before and After Wesley* in which he describes the savagery of the eighteenth century that is characterized by torture of animals for sport, bestial drunkenness of the populace, inhuman traffic of Africans, slavery, mortality of children, universal gambling obsession, the savagery of the penal system and penal code, prostitution of the theatre, lawlessness, superstition and lewdness, political bribery and corruption, ecclesiastical arrogance, insincerity and debasement rampant in the Church and State. The force behind the spirit and strategies of reformation is the Evangelical Revival.[36]

The critical question to be asked is *why*? Why is this movement able to transform the moral character of the general populace more than any movement in British history? For one reason, John Wesley is a preacher of the gospel and a prophet of social righteousness. The gospel declares that all creation comes from God with design and purpose; and despite the intervention of evil and the distortion of such Divine plans, the redemptive work of Jesus Christ destroys the work of evil and reconciles all creation unto God. It is to be assumed that such a revival of practical Christianity is based upon such a belief that God is involved in human affairs and that there is a clear understanding of Divine purposes and designs for all creation. A revival of such magnitude comprehends the dimensions and implications of evil and human depravity that contributes to the disintegration of society. More importantly, the authors of such a revival proclaim a gospel that demands active engagement and not passive escape.

In the United States, social involvement is the product of evangelical religion and evangelism. Charles G. Finney, a lawyer turned evangelist, and author of *Lectures on Revival of Religion*, believes that preaching the gospel

---

36 J. Wesley Bready, *England Before and After Wesley* (Sevenoaks: Hodder & Stoughton, 1939).

brings faith in Christ and a concern for reforms and revivals.[37] Finney is concerned that the gospel releases an impulse for social reforms. The emergence of the social gospel that is preached by Walter Rauschenbusch is in itself a reaction to passivity and negligence of the Church.[38] Rauschenbusch, a Professor of Church History at Rochester Seminary in New York from 1897 to 1917, believes that it is not a matter of getting individuals into heaven, but of transforming the life on earth into the harmony of heaven. While Rauschenbusch identifies the Kingdom of God with the reconstruction of society on a Christian basis and believes that human beings can establish the divine Kingdom themselves, the Evangelicals deny that the Kingdom of God is Christianized society. For them, the Kingdom is the divine rule in the lives of those who acknowledge Christ. It must be received, entered, or inherited by faith in the Lord Jesus. Those who are "born again" are members of a new community of the Lord Jesus who are called to exhibit the ideals of His rule in the world as an alternative social reality. Even though there are alleged errors in Rauschenbusch's theology, there is an underlying belief that the terms "influence" and "occupy" are an expression of active stewardship.[39]

The idea of a worldview being influenced by a concept of the Kingdom of God is presented by Grace Halsell in her book *Prophecy and Politics: Militant Evangelists on the Road to Nuclear War*. Halsell writes that a worldview that is influenced by a belief that the Bible predicts the imminent Second Coming of Jesus Christ after a period of global nuclear warfare, natural disasters, economic collapse and social chaos, influences American politics during the Ronald Reagan era.[40] The possibility that God foreordains a nuclear war and the belief by political officials in the feasibility of such a crisis greatly discourages any type of arms negotiations. Halsell poses the possibility that if a nuclear crisis occurs, a political leader with such

---

37   Dennis Carroll, Bill Nicely, and L.G. Parkhurst, Jr, Finney's *Systematic Theology: New Expanded Edition* (Minneapolis: Bethany House Publishers, 1994).

38   Walter Rauschenbusch, *Christianity and the Social Crisis* (London: Macmillan, 1907).

39   Walter Rauschenbusch, *A Theology for the Social Gospel* (New York: Macmillan, 1917).

40   Grace Halsell, *Prophecy and Politics: Militant Evangelists on the Road to Nuclear War* (Westport, Connecticut: Lawrence Hill & Company, 1986).

a worldview may be willing to "push the red button" and thereby believe that he is helping God in a Biblical, foreordained plan for the End of Time.

If a worldview answers the basic questions of why are we here, who is in charge, and how much authority do we have, then it should influence the attitude and activity of the Church toward the world. This can be seen whenever the Church gets involved politically and there are protests from within its ranks and from outside. The critical question is why? Is the world divided into a sacred and secular sphere with God only being concerned with the sacred? The opposition believes that the Church should avoid politics because religion (sacred) and politics (secular) do not mix. A worldview that affirms a God of creation, but not a God that is involved in the ongoing moral and social welfare of the world, will be involved in humanitarian work, especially in medical and educational programs, but not in political activity. Politics denotes the life of the city (polis) and the responsibilities of the citizens (polites). It is the concern of the whole of life in human society. Politics is the art of living together in community. Its narrow definition is the science of government. It is this view that defines politics as the development and adoption of specific policies with a view of their becoming legislation.

Luther in his "two kingdoms" approach seems to project a political concept of Divine authority in which the state is God's delegated authority to restrain evil and promote the righteousness of God. Since all authority comes from God, the state is a divine institution to promote the righteousness of God and governmental leaders should exercise their stewardship according to Biblical truth.[41]

It may be asked if Jesus is involved in politics. In the sense that politics is the science of government, He is not. He never forms a political party, adopts a political program or organizes a political protest. He does not run for a political office. Yet in a true sense, because He knows that all authority is given unto Him and that He has absolute dominion over the sacred, secular, and all forms of evil, His whole ministry is political. He sends His disciples into the world (secular) to transform it and not to escape from it.

---

41   Martin Luther, *The Bondage of the Will*, quoted in Paul Althaus, *The Theology of Martin Luther*, trans. Robert C. Schultz (Philadelphia: Fortress Press, 1966). P. 163.

He announces the Kingdom of God as a whole new existence of values and standards. Since His announcements are validated by the manifestations of supernatural power over all the consequences of evil, the Kingdom of God is the introduction of righteousness, joy, and peace into a disordered and fragmented society.

Once again, the worldview answers the basic question of who is in charge, but it also establishes the dimension of strategic responses toward the world. For example, the relation between social service and social action is influenced by a worldview. Social service includes relieving human need, philanthropic activity, ministry to individuals and families, and works of mercy. Social action involves removing the cause of human need, political and economic activity, seeking to transform the structures of society, and the quest for justice. Socio-political action looks beyond the persons to the structures; beyond the rehabilitation of prison inmates to the reform of the prison system; beyond caring for the poor to removing and even transforming the economic system and the political system; beyond improving factory conditions to securing a more participatory role for the workers; and beyond rehabilitation of prison inmates to the form of the prison system. Both the symptoms and the causes are addressed.

A Biblical worldview must express the difference between "escape" and "engagement." It demonstrates the belief that God is involved with humanity; that Divine plans and purposes are known; and that there are proper strategies for redeemed humanity to respond to such revelation. As aforementioned, it eliminates the boundary between the "sacred" and the "secular."

In the Scripture, the people of God are commanded to execute righteousness. Judges are commanded to show no partiality in mediating a case, "for the decision of justice belongs to God" (Deut. 1:17). When justice is properly executed, people are the agents of the divine will (Isaiah 59:15-16). Biblical righteousness means the vindication by God of those who cannot receive their own rights. Biblical righteousness is creative righteousness in the sense that it intends to restore the poor, oppressed, the misfits, and the disinherited their privileges of economic and political rights. A classic example is the law of Jubilee in which the restoration of equality is administered every fifty years. All lands, whether sold or foreclosed, are to be returned to their original owners (Lev. 25:25-28, 35-36; Deut. 10:18; Isaiah 58:7).

Social righteousness is a topic that is common throughout the prophetic literature and the New Testament writings. It is regarded as indispensable to faith, for without it all other forms of religious practices are worthless. Notice the followings references:

1. *He upholds the cause of the oppressed and gives food to the hungry. The Lord sets prisoners free, the Lord gives sight to the blind, the Lord lifts up those who are bowed down, the Lord loves the righteous. The Lord watches over the alien and sustains the fatherless and widow, but He frustrates the ways of the wicked.* (Psalm 146:7-9)

2. *The Most High is sovereign over the kingdoms of men and gives them to anyone He wishes.* (Daniel 4:32)

3. *From heaven the Lord looks down and sees all mankind; from his dwelling place he watches all who live on earth; He who forms the hearts of all who considers everything they do.* (Psalm 33:13-15)

4. *I hate, I despise your feast, and I take no delight in your solemn assemblies. Even though you offer me your burnt offerings and cereal offerings, I will not accept them and the peace offering of your fatted beast I will not look upon. Take away from me the noise of your song to the melody of your harps, I will not listen. But let justice roll down like waters, and righteousness like an ever flowing stream.* (Amos 5:21-24)

5. *With what shall I come before the Lord, and bow myself before God on high? Shall I come before him with burnt offering, with calves of year old? Will the Lord be pleased with a thousand rams, with ten thousand of rivers of oil? Shall I give my first born for my transgression, the fruit of my body for the sin of my soul? He has showed you, O man, what is good and what the Lord requires of you but to do justice, and to love kindness and to walk humbly with your God.* (Micah 6:6-8)

6. *To do righteousness and justice is more acceptable to the Lord than sacrifice.* (Psalm 21:3)

Jesus teaches that the resolution of a conflict between neighbors must precede the offering of gifts on the altar of sacrifice (Matt. 5:23-24). The teachings and practices of Jesus relate to the traditions of the prophets when

He rebukes the Scribes, Pharisees, and hypocrites for their unrighteousness and lack of mercy (Matt.23:23). Even the writings of Paul connect social righteousness with Christian responsibility to the poor (2 Cor. 9:9-10; 1 Tim. 6:17-19). It appears that righteousness is not simply a theory, but it is to be demonstrated in both its ethical and practical dimensions. It relates to the distribution of wealth, income, punishment, rewards, liberties, rights, duties, opportunities, and authority. Righteousness is to be expressed in every sphere of practical life.

In every society, the laws, legislation, institutions, and organizations display the values and respect for all aspects of life. For example, the laws of a society protect the educational system that administers rights, privileges, and quality. Legislation is enacted to preserve the social welfare of the citizens. Institutions and organizations are established to insure that succeeding generations are taught to preserve and emulate these same values. Likewise, these same systems can display a knowledge and respect for God when righteousness is understood and implemented.

Yet, what is to be done when a society is organized upon principles and practices contrary to the righteousness of God? What is the mission and responsibility of the Church toward such a society? In 1987, my wife and I were invited to be guest speakers in South Africa by the largest Pentecostal Denomination in the country. It was the first interracial conference sponsored by the organization during the apartheid regime of injustice, oppression, and inequality. It was commonly known that this Pentecostal organization did not condone the involvement of its churches in the political and social issues of the country. The leaders stood against the "politicizing of the church" and restricted their mission to the work of individual salvation. That is, the church communicated the gospel in a way that demanded decisions and generated converts, but the church was not to be involved in the redirection of the political or social life of the country. Although conversion is a redirection of the life of an individual, a deliverance from self, a break with the world, and the increase awareness of moral responsibility, the leaders did not believe that the church was to be involved in the socio-political affairs of South Africa.

The crisis of their worldview was influenced by their concept of the Kingdom of God. For them, God rules in the spirit and not through institutions or political organizations. Hence, they separated the sacred sphere of the Church form the secular sphere of politics, laws, and legislation. The Kingdom was a future reality that was to be realized at the Second Coming of the Lord Jesus. Therefore, it was spiritual, future, heavenly, and did not involve this present world. The world, according to their view, was under the judgment of God and the signs of this divine judgment were to be seen in the turmoil, oppression, injustice, divisions, wars, and the forms of evil.

During our 30 days of meetings in their conference, my wife and I taught and dialogued on the ethical and moral demands of the Kingdom of God upon the Church. We made reference to our local church in Decatur, Georgia (Chapel Hill Harvester Church), with its numerous outreach ministries and its theology of influence. During one of the night sessions, I gave prophetic words concerning South Africa. There was an overwhelming positive response from the 5,000 leaders in attendance. The prophetic words are briefly summarized as follows:

> O South Africa! You are jewels in the hand of the Lord. Although today you are the scourge of nations because of your problems, there is coming a day when the nations when come to your shores to see what you have done by the power of God!

Immediately at the end of the meeting, the news media converged upon us with questions. They asked if we were politicians or ambassadors from America. They were anxious to know the source of our authority to make those pronouncements. Interviews with the media provided us the opportunity to express the principles and practices that relate the Kingdom of God, a worldview, the Church, and a nation together. After the meetings, reports were written in the local papers about our comments and they eventually reached the political sector of the country. In fact, a recorded tape of one of our messages was personally given to the president of the country by a governmental official who was in attendance during one our meetings.

During a time of dialogue in the Bible School of that denomination, the students and teachers were suddenly alarmed by the arrival of several members of the African National Congress (ANC). One of the members of the ANC party asked permission to make a statement and pose a question. His statement denounced the government and the oppression that was rampant in the country and he justified violence as a strategy employed by the Lord Jesus when He drove the money changers from the temple. He asked us to state our position regarding the apartheid regime and the responsibility of the Church. His statements and questions were an expression of a growing movement supported by the tenets of Liberation Theology, which was threatening the classical Pentecostal's position of non-involvement. Our presentation of the ethical and moral demands of the Kingdom of God, a worldview, and the role of the Church were a great surprise to him. For the first time he was made aware of an alternative theology of influence capable of giving rise to strategies for socio-political reformation without physical violence.

As aforementioned, God is moral and just and He expects His delegated authorities to be moral and just. Righteousness is not simply to be limited to religious matters but it is to be demonstrated in all human affairs. The Church represents the conscious of God in the world. The Scripture presents human government not only as existing, but as deriving its authority and right to administer justice and protection, from God. Human government is part of the moral government of God (Dan. 2:21; 4:17, 25; 5:21; Rom. 13:1-7; Tit. 3:1; 1 Pet. 2:13, 14). Any society or culture that claims to honor God will demonstrate such honor in the principles and tenets that support the administration of its laws, legislation, institutions, and organizations. God continues to impart concepts and models of righteousness through the Church that are to influence the patterns of life in the world (John 3:16-21; Matt. 13:28; Luke 4:18).

Before ending this section, it is important to explore a worldview that properly addresses the issue of evil and its influence or limitations upon the attitude and the behavior of the Church and its membership in an unbelieving world. The facts and benefits of redemption through Jesus Christ and the proposition that Satan is a defeated foe with limited jurisdictional authority in the world presents an exciting prospect for fulfilling the great commission (Matt. 28:18-20; Mark 16:15-18). It also presents a compelling argument for defining concepts of "spiritual warfare" in world evangelism, especially among Charismatic and Pentecostal circles.

First of all, the idea of evil is complex. Perhaps the question of its origin is not quite as compelling today as the question of its character and influence. There are some basic questions to be addressed. For example, how powerful is the devil? What are the "wiles" of the devil? Is there such a thing as two competing spiritual forces of good and evil at work in the universe? What is the nature of spiritual warfare in connection with world evangelism? Finally, what is the authority and implications of the redemptive work of Jesus Christ?

Perhaps a brief history is relevant here, since evil is viewed as something that is either nonexistent, existent but limited, or existent but purely psychological. In creation, the serpent persuades the woman and ultimately the man through the use of question, suggestion, and the slander of God to disobey divine mandates (Gen. 1-3). This original encounter is verbal and therefore psychological since it does not involve a violation or intrusion of the person of the woman with some spirit. This may provide some evidence that the origination and promotion of evil is through the use of ideas, thoughts, convictions, and beliefs that ultimately influences behavior. It is the persuasion and the rationalization of alternatives or choices that are contrary to Divine knowledge and purposes. In the garden, the serpent never suggests that God is non-existent. In fact, the serpent acknowledges Divine power with the statement that "God doth know that in the day ye eat, thereof, then your eyes shall be opened, and ye shall be as gods, knowing good and evil" (Gen. 3:5). In this statement, there is the subtle slander of God in the suggestion that some privilege is being denied the humans that they rightly deserve. There is also the suggestion that if human initiative is taken, then there will be some immediate results. Such slander and suggestion awakens desires and ambitions in the mind of the woman and she is persuaded to believe a lie. The effect of this deception and subsequent rebellion and fall is the introduction of devastating consequences (Gen. 3:15-19; Rom. 5:18-19). These consequences are progressive and comprehensive throughout all generations (Rom. 5:12; 18-19; 8:20-21).

This idea of original sin is pervasive and violates Divine intentions (1 Cor. 2:6-8). It influences the ideas, convictions, decisions, customs, values, traditions, and institutions of all humanity. It is seen to intrude into the social order and in the lives of individuals through economic exploitation, oppression, hoarding of wealth from the poor, and even the promotion of insensitivity to all forms of social evils (Jam. 2:2-9, 13-18; 5:1-6). In essence, the consequences of this original transgression are progressive and comprehensive throughout all succeeding generations.

Something must be said about the unseen world of spirits. The belief in angels is a Biblical concept that perhaps can be seen also in Hellenist cultures. It is believed that God's care and control of everything in creation from stars to nations is through angelic agents. Each of the succeeding nations has its own angelic ruler and guardian as seen in Daniel where Michael is a celestial prince over Israel. He contends with the custodian of Persia and Greece (Dan. 10:5-14).

This Biblical theme of angelic supervision is also prevalent in most Jewish apocalyptic literature (2 Enoch 19:4-5). Angels are appointed over seasons, years, rivers, seas, vegetation, and over every living thing. Hence, in the New Testament, powers and principalities are angelic beings that exhibit influence in the social order (1 Cor. 2:8; 2 Cor. 2:11; Eph. 2:1-2; 6:11-12; 1 John 4:1-5; 2 Thes. 2:3-4; 1 Tim. 4:1-5). Since government plays a significant role in the control of human life, it is not surprising that it is believed that celestial beings are charged with the control of good government of the world (2 Enoch 19:2).

In the New Testament, evil powers are fallen spirits (Luke 10:18; Rev. 12:12). They are linked with Satan (Eph. 2:2; 6:11-12), but Christ triumphs over them (Matt. 12:28; Col. 2:15; 1 John 3:8). They use their authority over the governments to attack Christians by working through political and social bodies (Rom. 8:35-39).

The idea of a personal devil is indicated in the Scripture (Luke 22:3; Acts 5:3; 1 Cor. 5:5; 2 Cor. 12:7; 1 Thes. 2:18; 1 Tim. 1:20). The account of Job reveals that Satan is on restricted business in the earth and is permitted to attack his objects (Job 1:7-8). Sickness, poverty, and even death are at his disposal (Matt. 9:32-33; 12:22; 17:14-18; John 10:10). Daniel prays in earnest and is eventually notified by an angel that his prayers are initially answered when he prays, but the response is hindered by the "Prince of Persia" (Dan. 10:12-13). Israel encounters deprivation and defeat whenever they rebel against the Lord and emulate the idolatrous practices of heathen nations (Psalm 106). An evil spirit comes upon Saul after his rebellion (1 Sam. 15:16; 18:10; 19:9). The Lord puts a lying spirit in the mouths of false prophets to deceive Ahab (2 Chr. 18:4-21). It is Satan that provokes David to number Israel against the counsel of the Lord (1 Chr. 21:1), and it is Satan that directs Ananias and Sapphira to lie to the Holy Ghost (Acts 5:1-10).

In the New Testament, the interactions between Jesus with Satan are recorded (Luke 4:1-13). Demons are cast out of people with the verbal command of the Lord Jesus (Matt. 17:18; Mark 1:25; 9:25; Luke 4:35). The presence of the Kingdom is demonstrated by the authority over Satan (Matt. 12:28; Luke 11:20). Evil spirits are exorcised from demoniacs and the spirits are permitted to enter animals (Mark 5:1-14). Satan is eulogized with the words that he "falls from heaven as lightening" indicating the extent of his loss of power (Luke 10:18). Jesus gives the disciples power over the devil and over all of his works (Luke 9:1; Mark 16:17-18). John states that Jesus comes into the world to destroy the "works of the devil" and New Testament believers are given authority over such evil (1 John 3:8; 4:4).

The apostles are not overly preoccupied with the devil although they do not deny his existence (Acts 5:3; 26:18; Rom. 16:20; 1 Cor. 7:5; 2 Cor. 2:11; 12:7; 1 Thes. 2:18; 1 Pet. 5:8). They encounter evil often as an incarnation of disputes, beliefs, ideas, convictions, philosophies, knowledge, and practices that are working in the hearts and minds of people (Acts 8:9-11; 13:6-11; 2 Cor. 4:4; 10:4-6; Col. 2:18-23; 2 Pet. 3:1-4). The deception of Ananias and Sapphira is addressed by Peter as being the work of Satan (Acts 5:1-10). Paul and Silas encounter a young girl who is possessed with a spirit of divination (Acts 16:16). Paul and Barnabas engage a sorcerer named Elymas who seeks to turn a potential convert away from the faith (Acts 13:6-11). Paul, full of the Holy Ghost, looks on the false prophet and pronounces judgment: "O full of all deceit and all fraud, you son of the devil, you enemy of all righteousness, will you not cease perverting the straight ways of the Lord? And now, indeed, the hand of the Lord is upon you, and you shall be blind, not seeing the sun for a time" (Acts 13:6-11). The sorcerer is struck blind.

It is Paul who insists that there is no ignorance of the devil and his tactics (2 Cor. 2:11). He recognizes that Alexander the coppersmith (2 Tim. 4:14), Hymenaeus and Philetus (2 Tim. 2:17-18), false prophets, and "men of corrupt minds, disapproved concerning the faith" (2 Tim. 3:8), are all the consequences of the "messenger of Satan" that is released to buffet him (2 Cor. 12:7-10). However, there is never a mentioning of warring with Satan in prayer or even a constant battle with Satan for the souls of people. The resistance to Paul's ministry to the Gentiles in an unbelieving world is described in terms of tribulations, needs, distresses, stripes, imprisonment, tumults, dishonor, and other challenges (2 Cor. 6:4-10). Paul stands in opposition to false doctrines and philosophies and refers to them as "strongholds," "arguments," and "every high thing that exalts itself against the knowledge of God" (2 Cor. 10:4-6; Gal. 3-5; 2 Thes. 2:1-15; 1 Tim. 4:1; 2 Tim. 3:1-17). It appears that evil is incarnate in the unbelieving world in the form of philosophies, doctrines, and practices of religious systems, but the apostles give no indication of it having any dominance over their message or over their ministry (2 Cor. 2:14; 2 Tim. 4:17-18).

If Satan is an eternally defeated foe and if Jesus Christ "disarmed powers and principalities" and "destroyed the works of the devil," then the world is viewed from a very different perspective. If the Kingdom of God is the involvement of Divine power and authority in human affairs and the promotion of Divine purposes and plans, then the response of the Church must be aggressive and not passive. In fact, the idea of "spiritual warfare" must be viewed as the aggressive activities on the Church to evangelize the world.

Bishop Michael Reid presents an exhaustive treatise of the entire concept of Strategic Level Spiritual Warfare (SLSW) in which he explores the biblical concept of warfare with some of the contemporary trends in religious thought. His work is an evaluation of the biblical, theological, and historical bases for the current teaching on SLSW and a review of the contemporary literature on the subject.[42]

Dr. T.L. Osborn, who is one of the most effective evangelists of this century and who preaches to millions in over 80 nations, still demonstrates that the gospel is the power of God unto salvation.[43] He contends that the misrepresentation of Scriptural references to "weapons of our warfare" (2 Cor. 10:4), "whole armor of faith" (Eph. 6:11-18), "fight the good fight of faith" (1 Tim. 6:12), and "wiles of the devil" (Eph. 6:11), serve as the basis of the distorted concept of spiritual warfare in global evangelism.[44] The benefits of the truths of the redemptive victory of Jesus Christ offer

---

42 Michael S.B. Reid, *Strategic Level Spiritual Warfare: A Modern Mythology?* (Fairfax, Va.: Xulon Press, 2002).

43 T.L. Osborn, *Soul Winning: A Classic on Biblical Christianity,* (Tulsa, Ok.: Osborn Publishers, 1963).

44 T.L. Osborn, *The Message That Works,* (Tulsa, Ok.: Osborn Publishers, 1997.)

tremendous implications (1 Cor. 15:57; Col. 2:13-15). Spiritual warfare is not a military conflict that is waged in prayer, but it is the strategies and tasks of the Christian witness in action to win the lost.

Dr. Osbom describes spiritual warfare as a conflict waged on the feet and not on the knees.[45] It is the battle to get the attention of the masses of unconverted people who are distracted with all kinds of ideas, beliefs, and convictions. It is finding ways to acquire finances and other resources necessary to initiate and sustain the cost of world evangelism. It is the struggle to overcome the negative concepts and the obstacles to the gospel while persuading people to believe Christ and what He has accomplished. It is the persistence against all odds to reach the lost and to demonstrate the mission of the Church. Satan holds legal dominion over unbelievers, but when they hear and believe the gospel that dominion is broken. This is not accomplished through "warfare prayer" but through the communication of the truth. The "weapons of our warfare" are the gospel and the truths of the redemptive work of Jesus Christ. It is the declaration and the performance of these redemptive facts in an unbelieving world. Like the farmer who plows the soil, plants the seed, and expects a harvest, spiritual warfare is preparing the soil (minds, attitudes, and beliefs of the unconverted world), planting the seed (the gospel and all of its implications), and reaping the harvest (deliverance from all evil and translation into the Kingdom of God).

Spiritual warfare is to be viewed as a strategy to "police the principles and the practices" of the Kingdom of God. That is, the principles, tenets, and concepts that serve as the foundation of God's righteous government are to be preserved and implemented. The Scripture express the existence of "doctrines of devils," 'vain philosophies," and "arguments and every high thing that exalts itself against the knowledge of God" (1 Tim. 4:1; Col. 2:8; 2 Cor. 10:5). Hence, true warfare is not simply "beating the air," but it is contending for the faith once delivered to us. Warfare is the publication of materials and the use of the media to present Biblical points of view to both the believing and the unbelieving world. It is also ensuring that the jurisdictional authority of the Church is not limited simply to sacred spheres of human existence but involve all areas of life.

---

45   Lecture notes on *Prayer, Demons, and Global Evangelism* by T.L. Osbom at Peniel Church, London, 2002.

The implications of these concepts of faith, dominion, evil, and evangelism greatly influence a worldview. If the idea of evil is to kill, steal, and destroy, then the reality of righteousness is to save, give, and build. The world is to be viewed as a moral factor with all of its ideas, concepts, values, wisdom, knowledge, laws, institutions, and organizations. The world is not to be avoided or escaped. The Lord Jesus prays that His disciples be not taken out of the world but that they should be kept from the evil (John 17:15). The world is to be engaged and influenced by the redeemed community. The idea of justice and righteousness is more than a theory or an ideology for it must be practiced. Even though evil exist as an incarnation in individuals and in the systems of the world, the Kingdom of God provides the mandate, authority, and the power for the redeemed community to restore Divine purposes and intentions in the lives of individuals and also in the laws, legislation, institutions, and governments of the world. This also answers the basic questions posed at the beginning of this section. In the next section we explore the role of the Church based upon its worldview and its concept of the Kingdom of God.

Practical Implications

In this section, we wish to examine briefly the implications of a theology of the Kingdom of God upon the attitude and behavior of the Church and its ministry. Perceptions of the Kingdom of God are translated into principles, practices, and priorities that ultimately function as the interpretative concept that influences the life and activities of the Church. Such perceptions influence the infrastructures, evangelism, outreach ministries, coalitions, and even the associations of the local Churches.

It may be said that evangelism is one of the central functions of the Church, but not its total work. Evangelism is the communication of the Gospel in a manner that commands individual decisions. Such conversion is a redirection of a life and an increased awareness of the purposes and intentions of God. Hence, evangelism contributes to the moral transformation of any society since people are God's vehicles of such transformation. No society of social and political righteousness can be sustained with a declining foundation of faith and the consciousness of God. However, to assume that evangelism is the only true strategy for global transformation is a faulty position. The spiritual transformation of individuals must be accompanied with strategies for their intellectual transformation. This comes about through instruction and experiences that expose the reality of evil and righteousness and the individual's authority and responsibility to influence his/her environment. Such a transformation is accomplished through the availability of concepts, ideas, values, and principles that are internalized and implemented by each convert.

The world must be viewed as a moral factor and not simply as a sphere of terrestrial and celestial bodies. The world, morally speaking, is humanity organizing its life apart from the knowledge, purposes, and intentions of God. It is human counsel attempting to contradict Divine counsel (Psalm 2). The breakdown of moral values in a society is the direct result of unregenerate man's efforts to throw off the restraints of God and to remove the boundaries that are established by Divine consciousness.

When Divine rationality is abandoned and there is the removal of absolute principles from the laws and legislation of a society, then there is the occurrence of heresies, divisions, schisms, racism, euthanasia, abortion, genocide, and all other practices based upon consensus judgment and relativism (Rom. 1:16-32). Such sustained rebellion incurs the consequences of spiritual blindness in which humanity is unable to recover itself without the mediation of the Gospel (Rom. 1:18-32; 2 Thes. 2:9-12).

The truths of God endure throughout every generation (Psalm 100:5). There is such a thing as absolute truth, thought, principle, law, rule, concept, and value. Methods or strategies may change with each succeeding generation, but the underlying truths must remain. These irrefutable truths and concepts relate to the government of God and are applicable to every culture, society, country, and generation. It is this universality and transcendence of the Kingdom of God that declares that there are enduring concepts such as the sovereignty of God; the value of human life; the respect for law and order; and the brotherhood of all humankind.

As already mentioned, if individual evangelism is viewed as the chief responsibility of the Church and if the world is not viewed as a moral factor, then priority is given to the numerical growth of the local Church and no concern is given to the socio-political welfare of the society. The local Church influenced by such a perspective will develop the spiritual life of its members through intramural programs that focus on family life, inner healing, deliverance, prayer, and even schools of theological training. Even though such efforts to develop the individual spiritual lives of the members are commendable, the members of the Church never realize their stewardship responsibilities. The lawyers, educators, entertainers, scientists, athletes, politicians, entrepreneurs, students, and all other members never realize their stewardship responsibility to influence the sphere of their personal involvement. The members are encouraged to "do the work of an evangelist" and offer personal witness to the unsaved with the hope of converting them to the faith, but they will rarely explain how a Christian is to be "salt and light" in the world (2 Tim. 4:5; Matt. 5:13, 14).

When the Kingdom of God is viewed as only being spiritual and not involved with the "carnal affairs" (education, politics, entertainment, economics, science, commerce, laws, etc.), then the reign of God is understood to exert its influence only in the spirit realm and not through the governmental and social structures of the society. The grace of God is not seen to operate in arts, science, technology, entertainment, education, or athletics. The Church, with its preaching, teaching, and outreach ministry, becomes a "cultural critic" rather than a "cultural architect." Improper concepts of jurisdictional authority that limit the work of the Church to the sacred spheres and exclude its involvement in the secular spheres of human existence will greatly hamper the work of the Church. When there are strong convictions that a "new heaven and new earth" (2 Pet. 3:13) means the literal annihilation of the present terrestrial and celestial bodies, then the stewardship of the earth is viewed as "polishing the brass on a sinking ship" and there is an obvious pessimism that invades the Church.

The Kingdom of God relates to laws, rules, and legislation. Even though it is not limited to politics and government, its influence is not separate from such aspects of human life. The government of God exerts its influence in redemption (individual salvation) and providence (cosmic order). Although the salvation of the individual may be the center of God's will, it is not the circumference. The providential dimension of the Kingdom is expressed in the power of God to rule over individuals, nations, circumstances, and all the created order.

There is a distinction between the Kingdom and the Church. While the Kingdom relates to laws, rules, and governments, the Church is identified with meetings, worship, and membership. The Church is the redeemed community serving as the executive representative of the power, principles, priorities, and practices of the Kingdom. It is the Church that reveals the "manifold wisdom of God" to powers and principalities. It is through the Church that God imparts concepts and models of righteousness that serve as a template for society. It is the Church that executes dominion over the community of evil.

Any theology of the Kingdom of God must address three fundamental concerns:

1. The involvement of God in human affairs.

2. The restoration of earthly things according to the heavenly pattern.

3. The strategies for human response to the revelation of God.

These three concerns encapsulate, to some degree, the reality of the Kingdom of God in its multiple polarities of time (past, present and future), space (heaven and earth), and dimension (spiritual and natural). The involvement of God in human affairs is the expression of His sovereign rule over all people, circumstances, times, and season. It is God at work in redemption and providence. The restoration of earthly things according to the heavenly pattern is the revelation of the original purposes of God in the creation of all things. It is the will of God demonstrated in creation, organization, and maintenance of all order. The strategies of human response to such revelation are the gifts, callings, ideas, words, principles, practices, methods, devises, schemes, institutions, organizations, and structures necessary for such accomplishments. It is the understanding of the person, character, and way of the Lord in the sacred, secular, and civil sphere of human existence.

Our initial goal is to demonstrate how the mission of the Church is influenced by an understanding of the demands, responsibilities, and privileges of the Kingdom of God. Our chief objective is to develop an attitude of tolerance among the various factions created by the different views of the Kingdom with the hope of reconciling the differences. In recognition of the polarities of the Kingdom and the variety of views regarding its nature and implications, there is the hope of creating a format for the convergence of these various ideas, expectations, and convictions. In our final sections, we intend to examine the multiple polarities (individual, corporate, spiritual, natural, heavenly, earthly, past, present, and future) of the Kingdom of God and present a model of convergence.

CHAPTER 8

$\mathcal{D}$ifferent
$\mathcal{V}$iews

Some may say the Kingdom is a present reality, manifested only spiritually in the hearts of believers, or as the Church (Luke 17:21). Meanwhile, others await its future fulfillment in the Second Coming (Luke 17:24). Regardless of the view taken in reference to the Kingdom of God, there is no disagreement about its existence. Still, there are a variety of opinions regarding its nature, present implications, and time of its appearance. The polarities of the Kingdom breed confusion to the natural mind when efforts are made to circumscribe it into a singular concept. It can be seen that the Kingdom is divine action, but it is also human participation (Luke 19:11-27; Matt. 6:33; Col. 4:11); it is in some dimension now, but it is also future (Mark 1:15; Matt. 6:10); it is spiritual, but it is also natural (1 Cor. 15:50; John 18:36); and it is heavenly with earthly implications (John 18:36; Matt. 25).

With these thoughts in mind, let us explore three belief systems and their implications upon the attitude and operational behavior of the universal Church in its local settings.[46] The categories are separated into the following:

---

46   Howard Synder, *Models of the Kingdom*, Nashville:Abingdon Press, 1991.

1. The Kingdom of God as future, spiritual, and heavenly (Matt. 6:10; Luke 17:21; John 18:36; 1 Cor. 15:50)

2. The Kingdom of God as present, physical, and earthly (Mark 1:15; Luke 4:18-21; Col. 4:11)

3. The Kingdom of God as present, future, spiritual, physical, earthly, and heavenly (Matt. 6:10; Mark l:15; Luke 4:18-21; John 118:36; 1 Cor. 15:50; Col. 4:11)

The Kingdom of God as Future, Spiritual, and Heavenly

The belief in a future hope and the expectation of "a new heaven and a new earth" (2 Pet. 3:13) as the final result of cosmic reconciliation is the foundation of this belief system. Even though the "present" aspect of the Kingdom is experienced in the First Coming of the Lord and in the outpouring of the Holy Spirit at Pentecost (Acts 3:19-21), the expectation of final judgment; the culmination of all evil and injustice; and the formation of a new creation (utopia) in which all the earth experiences peace, holiness, and happiness, is key in this system (Rom. 14:17; 1 Cor. I 15:24-25; 2 Thes. 1:5; 2 Tim. 2:12, 4:1, 18; Heb. 12:28; Rev. 11:15, 12:10, 20:1-6). Hence, there is a sense in which the "future" Kingdom is expressed as a single "crisis" event rather than a progressive transformation of all things.

The preaching and teaching ministry that supports this theology is evangelistic, world denying, and futuristic since it focuses upon the ultimate judgment and the final reconciliation of all things. Even though there is a constant reference to the consequences of the First Coming of Jesus, there is a significant emphasis on the Second Coming of Christ as the "blessed hope" and the "Day of the Lord" (Matt. 24:14; Luke 12:35-40; 17:20-37; 21:5-36; Acts 1:11; 1 Thess. 4:13-18; Titus 2:13). In essence, the burden of preaching is directed toward events to come rather than upon the benefits already achieved with the coming of the Lord and the outpouring of the Holy Spirit.

The promise of a "new heaven and a new earth" as foretold in Isaiah 11, 24:21-23, 65:11, and 66:22, and 2 Peter 3:10-13 supports the belief of a literal annihilation of celestial and terrestrial bodies. Such a belief also generates an apathy and complacency regarding the systems and structures of the world. Since the "fashions of this world are passing away" (1 Cor. 7:31), there is very little effort to influence the social and political environment of communities. Such an expectation of a literal annihilation promotes a radical individualism in members of the church to develop their individual callings and gifts of the Holy Spirit in the midst of a present world that is soon coming to an end (Isaiah 65:17; 2 Pet. 3:1-18). Such a preoccupation with a future inheritance and the "glory to be revealed" (Jam. 2:5; Col. 1:12), distorts the concept of ministry and creates "preachers" rather than "witnesses."

This preoccupation with the last days and a devaluation of the responsibility of believers to exercise stewardship in the secular sphere is one of the basic reasons motivating many professionals to abandon their occupations and become "full-time" ministers. Ministry is erroneously perceived as preaching in a local church, teaching the Bible, and going to the mission fields rather than exercising influence in the market places.

Historical support for this view is gleaned from Irenaeus and Tertullian. Irenaeus (c. 115-c. 202), the bishop of Lyons expresses a view of the Kingdom as the ultimate restoration and renewal.[47] Focusing on Romans 8 and the promises of God to Abraham, Irenaeus believes in a literal fulfillment of the biblical promises of the Kingdom in the future. He expresses the idea that creation will be restored to its original state; the meek will inherit the earth; and the created order will be made new and set free. Tertullian (c. A.D. 160-c. 225) identifies the practical significance of the Kingdom of God as it relates to the challenges of his day.[48] He believes that God reigns over all but that the decline of conditions in the world and the catastrophes are indications that the last days are at hand. Christians are pilgrims in this present world expecting the return of Christ and the

---

47   Irenaeus, *Against Heresies*, 32-33, in Richardson, *Early Christian Fathers*, pp. 391-94.

48   Tertullian, *Prescription Against Heretics*, 13, in the *Ante-Nicene Fathers*, eds. Alexander Roberts and James Donaldson (Grand Rapids: Eerdmans, 1976), 3:249.

coming of the Kingdom. As such, they enjoy heavenly blessings now as they deny themselves earthly ones for the sake of the Kingdom. However, Christians are to enjoy blessings of the Kingdom in another state in the millennium.[49] Tertullian's view of the Kingdom is present with a primary emphasis on the future.

This concept of the Kingdom of God generates a worldview that is pessimistic. It visualizes God reigning over all creation, but in a spiritual realm only. A critical verse is Luke 17:20-21 when Jesus says, "The Kingdom of God does not come with observation, nor will they say, 'See here!' or 'See there!' For indeed, the kingdom of God is within you." This verse serves as strong motivation for the belief that the Kingdom is limited to the rule of God in the hearts of believers who respond in devotion and obedience in the limited sphere of their lives. Since the focus of the Kingdom is on the interior life of the believer, there is very little participation with the external environment. In this view, the degeneration of the social order is evidence of God's judgment and there is very little motivation for the Christian to influence the order of the culture. Since the Kingdom is spiritual and a "non-material reality," the burden of faith in this concept is the salvation of souls, world evangelism, church growth, and not the restructuring of the world order. Also, as aforementioned, the focus upon the final reconciliation of all things and the promise of a "new heaven and a new earth" (2 Pet. 3:13) which comes in the future encourages a future hope but does not promote contemporary involvement in the surrounding culture.

Classical Pentecostalism represents an expectation of a new age of the Spirit. It places an emphasis on signs and wonders as a methodology for evangelism and church growth without grasping the complete thrust of church life and mission. The miraculous does not violate the natural means by which the church performs its mission through Christ in the world. To say that "the Kingdom of God is not in word but in power" (1 Cor. 4:20), is not an admission that all ministry is accomplished through the miraculous alone.[50] Indeed, miracles, signs, and wonders are viewed as a foreshadow-

---

49   Tertullian, *Against Marcion*, 3:25, in the *Ante-Nicene Fathers*, eds. Alexander Roberts and James Donaldson (Grand Rapids: Eerdmans, 1976), 3:342.

50   Ray S. Anderson, *The Praxis of Pentecost: Revisioning the Church's Life and Mission* (Downers Grove, II.: Inter Varsity Press, 1992), p.151.

ing and a promise of a coming universal redemption.[51] The gifts of the Spirit are viewed as eschatological signs in addition to being useful for the growth and witness of the church.[52]

Despite the strength of this view, it tends to separate the world into "sacred" and "secular" spheres. A key text is Roman 14:17: "For the kingdom of God is not meat or drink, but righteousness, peace, and joy in the Holy Ghost." Another verse is John 18:36: "My kingdom is not of this world." The sacred sphere is described as the spiritual dimension and relates to the experiences and practices of things of God (1 John 2:1517; 4:4-5). The secular sphere seems to relate to the natural and the carnal experiences and practices such as work, education, economics, science, politics, government, entertainment, commerce, sports, etc. Even though there is an effort to bring spiritual experiences of visions, dreams, revelations, and insights into the realm of the secular, there is still the preoccupation with this distinct difference between the two spheres.

The schools and seminaries that are influenced by this view find it difficult to integrate practical and "secular" matters into their teaching and training curriculum. Students are often equipped with significant knowledge of the Scriptures but find themselves deficient in application since they are taught that this present world is passing away or that politics, economics, commerce, law, athletics, and even science are spheres of human involvement that are in rebellion to God. Their spiritual knowledge is in a sense "world-denying" or "other-worldly" with very little value for the material world. Rather than influencing the market place through human involvement in every legitimate occupation, the students find themselves defending their convictions. In this sense, the Kingdom of God is viewed as an *antagonist and its citizens* are *cultural critics* rather than *cultural architects* who can influence the order of society.

As aforementioned, even though evangelism is a strong emphasis, a fatalistic attitude toward the world focuses most evangelistic efforts upon the

51 John Wimber with Kevin Springer, *Power Evangelism* (San Francisco: Harper & Row, 1986), p20.

52 D. William Faupel, *The Everlasting Gospel: The Significance of Eschatology in the Development of Pentecostal Thought* (Sheffield: Sheffield Academic Press, 1996), p. 40-43.

salvation of the individual rather than upon the transformation of the surrounding culture. Since this view is in a sense "world denying" all global reports of violence, war, poverty, racism, and all aspects of social decline are viewed as the fruits of rebellious people and evidence that the judgment is at hand. Hence, there is very little effort to transform the surrounding culture. Churches can inhabit communities that are experiencing social, political, and spiritual decline without educating its members in the art of influence. In fact, the strong emphasis on church schools and even the home school programs may at times appear as a strategy of separation and escape from the public school system.

Such a view of the Kingdom influences the shepherding emphasis of the Church. Since the redemptive aspect of the Kingdom of God (individual salvation) is emphasized above the providential aspect (cosmic rule), the government of the Church stresses those offices that directly influence the growth of the local congregation. Hence, the offices of pastor, teacher, and evangelist (missionary) are stressed in the leadership development phase. Apostolic and prophetic ministries may be acknowledged. Such a system develops preachers rather than cultural architects such as lawyers, politicians, educators, economists, scientists, entertainers, athletes, artists, and martyrs. Because this concept stresses the rule of God through the spirit, it neglects the sovereignty of God that is expressed in politics, law, economics, education, commerce, and other similar aspects. Hence, Bible School training may be so strongly encouraged that members are discouraged from pursuing training in "secular schools" that would equip them to become cultural stewards.

The Kingdom of God as Present, Physical, and Earthly

The implications of a theocracy and the lack of a distinction between the Church and the Kingdom of God are quite significant in this belief system. Here the kingdom of God is viewed as the visible, militant, triumphant, and institutional Church upon the earth in every generation. The reign of God is viewed as being now, earthly, physical and even practical through ministries of the Church and other delegated structures. The concepts of a "royal priesthood" (Heb. 12:22-28; 1 Pet. 2:5; Rev. 1:6; 5:10) and the church building being called the "House of God" all contribute to this idea of the work of the Kingdom and the work of the Church being synonymous. The admonition for Christians to pray for rulers and to influence them offers a belief in a theocratic understanding of the Kingdom (Rom. 13:1). Of course, the signs of the Kingdom of God are to be seen in the growth and success of the Church in world evangelism.

Such a theology describes the present rule and government of God through its structures of human government. The laws and values of the Kingdom of God provide for the values, priorities, and methods for the social, political, and economic structure of society. The Church under this theology actively engages in all of the governmental structures and organizations of society (Matt. 13:31-34; Rom. 13).

Since the Kingdom of God is viewed as present and not just future, and physical and not just spiritual, this theology presents the concepts of the Kingdom as principles of social reconstruction empowered by the doctrine of the Holy Ghost. Social programs that signify the removal of the boundary line between the sacred and secular spheres cause the Church to focus upon the poor, suffering, and the oppressed in society. The Gospel, or the Social Gospel as it is sometimes called, is viewed as the power of God to bring about a world of peace, justice, and righteousness now. This view proposes that there can be fair government and just social structures through the progressive rule of Christians in all areas of life (Isaiah 11:1-9, 42:1-7, 61:1-11; Matt. 5-7; Luke 6:20-26). According to this belief system, the Kingdom of God on earth can be a culture that is transformed by humanity organized according to the will of God.

The preaching and teaching that empowers this theology is evangelistic, contemporary, and solution-oriented. The Kingdom of God is a blueprint for transforming the world. The elimination of racism, divisions, injustice, lawlessness, and atheism are a strong focus of the proclamation ministry of the Church. Sin is viewed as a personal breach of the relationship between humanity and God. It is also viewed as an expression of individual irresponsibility for the stewardship of the world.

The church that is influenced by this theology focuses upon individual responsibility and the removal of the sacred/secular boundary. It addresses the poor, the depressed, and the victimized through the channels of laws and legislation. However, there is a tendency to fashion a Utopian attitude and the belief that society can be transformed simply through laws, legislation, and governmental structures alone. Herein lies the failure to comprehend the depravity of sin and the delicate balance that must be maintained between human effort and Holy Ghost dynamic. The reconstruction of this entire world through Biblical principles and the formation of a near Utopian society will not occur before the Second Coming of the Lord. In fact, there will still be "tares and wheat;" "sheep and goat nations;" and "wars and rumors of wars" (Matt. 13:25-30; 25:32-33; Mark 13:7).

The government of the Church, according to this concept, is pastoral and authoritative. The universal priesthood of the believer is subordinated to the centralized authority of a leadership hierarchy. In essence, there is a clear distinction made between the "clergy" and the "laity," and such a heavy authoritarianism tends to hinder the spiritual development of the people and create an unhealthy dependence upon leadership.

Since God rules over all things, can God's Kingdom provide the values and even the strategies for the social, political, and economic reorganizations of the present society? Can the rule of God in and through the structures of the church and human government have a significant influence in the world? If the church is viewed as the custodian of society and the representative of God's rule on earth, is it empty optimism to expect the "rule of the saints" through strategic structures? Can world evangelism and church growth be viewed as signs of Kingdom reality? These are critical questions to be addressed in this concept.

The Kingdom of God as Present, Future, Spiritual, Natural, Earthly, and Heavenly

This view represents a convergence, with modifications, of the aforementioned two systems. The implications of the Church as the representative of the authority and the government of the Kingdom of God are significant in this belief system. This theology views the Kingdom of God in its multiple polarities and clearly eliminates the boundary lines between the sacred and the secular spheres. There is a benevolent attitude toward the world in its state of estrangement from God. The world is viewed as being in need of a message, a model, and a demonstration of what righteousness, peace, and joy really are in the Holy Ghost. This theology views the Kingdom of God and the Church as distinct yet inseparable. The Church is called to influence the activities of the world through the proclamation and the demonstration of the principles and practices of the Kingdom of God. Solution-oriented ministry programs and collaboration with authorities in areas of government, commerce, education, science, social welfare, and other areas of human concerns are viewed as strategies of influence.

This theology influences the interpersonal relationships between other redeemed communities. There seems to be efforts to reconcile difference that exists between ministries based upon end-time beliefs, concepts of Church government, and other areas of doctrinal and practical differences. This effort toward theological and practical tolerance, while maintaining the fundamentals of the faith, seems to evolve from an understanding of the unity of the Church and the polarities of the Kingdom of God. The Church is one, for Christ is not divided.

The preaching and teaching of the Church influenced by such a theology is historical, contemporary, and anticipatory. It embraces the values and contributions of the historic Church even though it may disagree with some of the theology and governmental structures. It is contemporary because it is solution-oriented, practical, and applicable to the individual and the society. It is anticipatory since it recognizes the value and significance of the First Coming of Jesus Christ; the establishment of the Church; the incarnation of the Holy Ghost; and the significant factor of the Second Coming.

Its efforts of evangelism are both individual and cosmic. The salvation of the individual and the entire created order are both primary objectives. Both the redemptive and the providential aspects of the Kingdom of God are considered. God rules in the hearts of the Christians and He also rules the nations. This theology influences an evangelistic effort that presupposes that the knowledge of God and His will are socially relevant.

The message of the Gospel is not restricted to the spiritual and sacred compartments of life. It is relevant to politics, economics, commerce, education, athletics, entertainment, and science. Such a theology produces cultural architects and martyrs who seek to transform their environment. It encourages entertainers, athletes, lawyers, physicians, dentists, politicians, educators, scientists, and others to be stewards of their professions.

In its tolerance of theological differences and even contradictions among other Christian communities, the churches influenced by this theology tend to demonstrate a strong effort to discover "common ground." There is a deliberate motive in such a theological emphasis to view the world as the field with many different laborers who share some essential and common views, hopes, aspirations, and faiths in one true and living God. Nevertheless, they also have differences.

Since such a theology views the Kingdom of God as being restorative in its relationship to the present world order, there is a strong effort among such Churches to restore communities and human life. This is often demonstrated in its policies, practices, and programs for the restoration of individuals who fall short of the Biblical standards of ethics and morality. Sin is the contradiction of the will and the way of God. Sin is the activity of the human creature acting in a very inhuman manner. Yet, it is the work of the Church, as a therapeutic community, to heal the sick and to reconcile those who are estranged because of ethical and moral faults.

The government of the Church that is influenced by this theology strongly recognizes the universal priesthood of believers even though the five-fold ministries of apostle, prophet, pastor, teacher, and evangelist are usually established in the structure. The ecclesiastical structure is clearly defined while promoting the priesthood of every believer regardless of sex, race, age, and socioeconomic status. If all offices are not installed in the local Church, there is at least an external association with ministries that demonstrate those offices. For example, if the offices of apostle and even prophet are not active in every local Church, those same Churches are networked with apostolic or even prophetic ministries.

CHAPTER 9

Convergent Model

In the previous sections, we presented the idea that perceptions of the Kingdom of God are translated into principles, practices, objectives, and priorities that ultimately influence the life and activities of the Church. Even though there is a diversity of opinions regarding the Kingdom of God, all factions generated by this controversy agree on its existence but differ in their understanding of its nature, present implications, and time of its appearance. Considering such a divergence of opinions, can there be a convergence of such theological concepts and practices? Can there be a consolidation with modifications of the Catholic, Protestant, and Pentecostal traditions? Can the polarities of the Kingdom presented in the Scriptures be reconciled into a comprehensive system? If there is such a possibility, is there a contemporary church model?

In this section, an example of such a convergence is presented in the example of a Pentecostal/Charismatic Church that underwent a radical transformation in its theology and practices. The key factor that precipitated the convergence is the concept of the Kingdom of God. Our study begins with a seemingly traditional Charismatic/Pentecostal church in Decatur, Georgia, that expanded its borders beyond the beliefs, disciplines, and practices of its heritage.[53] Breaking with traditions, the leaders began a work in the inner city of Atlanta, where they emphasized the five-fold ministry (apostle, prophet, pastor, evangelist, and teacher), Holy Spirit dynamic, expressive worship, liturgy, and socially active ministry programs. A previously all-white fellowship was transformed into a multi-cultural congregation through the efforts of the leaders to reconcile the racial conflicts of the city. A neo-gothic cathedral provided the accommodation for a congregation of over 12,000 members to worship God in psalms, hymns, spiritual songs, and make melodies in their hearts (Eph. 5:19). It also demonstrated the implication of Kingdom theology upon church architecture and ministry.[54] This local congregation and church once called Chapel Hill Harvester Church became known simply as the Cathedral of the Holy Spirit.

The church underwent a significant change when some of its theological views and practices were modified.[55] Having long embraced the idea of the Kingdom of God as a future hope and the church as a colony of redeemed people awaiting their deliverance from this present world, Pastor Earl Paulk was overwhelmed by a dream that radically transformed his theology.[56] The significance of the First Coming of Jesus and the implications upon the life and ministry of the church took on a different meaning. First, while classical Pentecostalism may emphasize the Second Coming of the Lord as the supreme event to which all else is preparatory, the finished work of Jesus was given priority. Second, the gospel that was preached by Jesus and the apostles assumed a primary place in the preaching agenda of the church. Fresh revelatory meaning was given to such phrases as "thy kingdom come, they will be done on earth as it is in heaven" (Matt. 6:10); and "held in the heaven until the restitution of all things" (Acts 3:19-21). Attention was given to words such as "witness," "occupy," "disciple," "salt," and "light." The boundary between the sacred sphere of the Church and

---

53 Earl Paulk, *The Unfinished Course: The Inspiring Story of Earl Paulk* (Shippensburg, Pa.: Destiny Image Publishers, 2004).

54 Earl Paulk, *20/20 Vision: A Clear View of the Kingdom of God* (Atlanta: Kingdom Publishers, 1988).

55 Earl Paulk, *The Ultimate Kingdom: Lessons for Today's Christian From the Book of Revelation* (Atlanta: K Dimension Publishers, 1986).

56 Earl Paulk, *Held In The Heavens Until: God's Strategy For Planet Earth* (Atlanta: K Dimension Publishers, 1985).

the secular sphere of the world was erased, and the concept of a prophetic community was presented.[57] The church was no longer be a "cultural critic" that denounced the problems of war, crime, immorality, and disorganization in the world as simply expressions of Divine judgment against human rebellion.[58] Instead, the church is to be a "cultural architect," empowered by the Holy Spirit, to offer solutions through the proclamation and demonstrations of the principles of the Kingdom of God in the midst of a confused world. A theology of escape was exchanged for a theology of influence.[59] Instead of avoiding "secular occupations" such as law, politics, education, science, athletics, entertainment, and commerce, the members of the church were encouraged to assume their stewardship responsibilities in all of these areas.[60]

The church demonstrated the necessity of blending theological concepts with practical strategies through its education system. Education was viewed as an evangelistic strategy; consequently, a school of theology was established and opened to all. Its intent was not to simply produce preachers but to also equip the "laity" with the tools to transform their world through practical and applied theological instructions. An elementary and a high school were initiated that provided an opportunity to merge secular education with sound Biblical ideas. The majority of the school's graduates went to college.

In recognition of the historical and spiritual renewal of this century, the leadership of the church took deliberate steps to reconcile the various factions in the Body of Christ.[61] This effort to integrate the contribution of three streams of Christian traditions came to be known as a "convergence movement." These three streams included the Roman Catholic tradition

---

57 Earl Paulk, *The Prophetic Community: God Answers the Prayer of His Son* (Shippensburg, Pa.: Destiny Image Publishers, 1995).

58 Earl Paulk, *The Local Church Says Hell, No!: The Vision Of One Congregation Fighting The Enemy In His Own Backyard* (Atlanta: Kingdom Publishers, 1991).

59 Earl Paulk, *The Great Escape Theory* (Decatur, Georgia: Chapel Hill Harvester Church, 1988).

60 Earl Paulk and Daniel Rhodes, *A Theology for the News Millennium* (Atlanta: Earl Paulk Ministries, 2000).

61 Kirby Clements, *A Philosophy of Ministry* (Decatur, Ga.: Clements Family Ministry, 1995).

with its emphasis on orthodoxy and the importance of liturgy and sacraments; the Reformed tradition which stressed the centrality of the Scripture, personal faith, and the importance of the proclaimed Word of God; and the Pentecostal tradition which emphasized the baptism of the Holy Spirit as an experience and His ongoing ministry in the Church through the gifts. Faith, preaching, teaching, creeds, confessionals, expressive worship, ministration of the Holy Spirit, communion, water baptism, choreographed dancing, and dramatic presentations were skillfully integrated together with fixed liturgical elements. A Charismatic Mass was one of the three services offered on Sunday that provided for the corporate participation of the leaders and the congregation within a structured environment filled with order and spontaneous celebration.

In a further effort to bridge the gap between the Pentecostal/Charismatic liturgy and the historic liturgy, the leaders replaced their traditional neckties and blouses for clerical collars. While liturgy and vestments had served as a boundary line between the traditions, this represented another effort to demonstrate a respect for historic forms while maintaining the power and ministration of the Holy Spirit.

This merging of form and power had its challenges. While form has an element of predictability and inspiration, it possesses a great degree of spontaneity, the leadership constantly guarded against any competition between the ministry of the Holy Spirit and the order of the services. An order of service with a scheduled list of ministries such as songs, dances, dramatic presentations, announcements, and even the preaching of the Word were always subject to those unplanned events that were judged to spiritually inspire. It demonstrated that freedom and order are compatible experiences.

Sensing a need to expand knowledge and practice, dialogue was initiated between the modem Pentecostal/Charismatic Church and the historic Roman Catholic Church over matters of universal priesthood, the episcopacy, the sacraments, the "real presence," and the Lord's Table. An International Communion of Charismatic Churches was formed to provide a trans-denominational forum that facilitated the exchange of ministry resources, ideas, counsel, and spiritual direction among the leaders and churches represented. The Communion grew to over 6,000 ministries in Africa, Asia, Australia, Europe, South America, and North America. The late Archbishop Earl Paulk once presided over the trans-denomination-al and trans-cultural communion that maintained its headquarters at the Cathedral of the Holy Spirit.

The Cathedral organized conferences to teach and demonstrate the practical concepts of the Kingdom of God. Pastors and leaders from various denom-inations were attracted to the teachings, music, dramatic presentations, and the various ministry programs of the church. As a result, a network of churches was developed to provide a forum for the ongoing exchange of wisdom, counsel, and ministry resources. Its membership included leaders from within and without the Pentecostal and Charismatic ranks. This was done in recognition of the unity and diversity in the Body of Christ.

Since the concept of the Kingdom presented the world as the field of ministry, the teachings, publications, music, and dramatic presentations of the Cathedral were exported to other states, countries, and nations. A most notable example of this exported influence was recorded in a newspaper article describing the impact of the ministry in South Africa. The churches in South Africa during the reign of apartheid ignored politics and simply preached the Gospel. Facing pressures from an emerging Liber-ation theology and Black liberals who demanded radical pronouncements and racial equality, the churches became confused and had no theology that could offer a viable solution. However, some of the reluctant politi-cians and the charismatics began to think politically due to the influence of an American import called "Kingdom theology." Its main proponent, according to the article, was Archbishop Earl Paulk, who emphasized that the church should be socially relevant and challenge ungodly world systems.[62]

The church received awards from President George H. Bush for its trans-forming work in the inner city public housing. Because the boundary line between the sacred and the secular was erased, social programs were designed and operated by volunteer teachers, entrepreneurs, doctors, nurses, athletes, and lawyers who established a resident ministry in one of the largest housing projects in metro Atlanta. The influence of the church upon the lives of the residents and the social environment was so signif-

---

62   Bruce Barron, *The Charismatics Path to South African Brotherhood*, (New York: Wall Street Journal, 1987).

icant that the project captured the attention of the political community. Today, the project is used as a model for many other churches in which entire communities are adopted as fields of ministry.

A critical factor in the ministry of the Cathedral was the desire of its leader, Archbishop Paulk, to protect anointings and to restore people. Since Jesus comes to "seek and save that which was lost" (Luke 19:10), and "the sick have need of a physician and not the well" (Matt. 9:12), the Cathedral stood as a place of restoration for the oppressed, the estranged, the devalued, the misfits, the fallen, and all who have came short of the glory of God or who existed outside of the boundaries of cultural orthodoxy. A ministry philosophy was designed to address some of the most difficult social and spiritual problems. For example, a church sponsored adoption agency was initiated to facilitate the adoption of babies born out of wedlock. An Ovecomers Ministry was established to help those individuals who were struggling with any form of addiction. Counsel was provided for the restoration of people and leaders who experienced personal failures. Thanks to such efforts, there are many more productive citizens in the Kingdom of God today.

A significant principle in the philosophy of ministry of the Cathedral was the belief in the *ideal* and the *exception*. Creation established the ideal of Divine purposes, intentions, and functions, while sin initiated the perversion, or the exception to this ideal. Consequently, there was a consistent effort to preach and demonstrate the Divine ideal for contemporary people, institutions, organizations, governments, and laws, while ministering to the very individuals and systems that fell short of that ideal. There are irrevocable norms, values, and practices that are acceptable in any culture. There are also exceptions to these standards. For example, freedom, love, justice, equity, and peace may be ideals while oppression, hatred, injustice, discrimination, and war are exceptions. The Gospel is the declaration of the purposes and intentions of God for humanity and all creation. The Church is the representative of the consciousness of these Divine plans. Yet, what should be the response of the Church toward those individuals who fall short of these ideals? Should it condemn or excommunicate? After all, the standards of God are the measuring rod for all human existence. Still, there must be a ministering community able to restore. The Church is the therapeutic community where healing, deliverance, inspiration, reconciliation, and restoration occur. In recognition of this fact, the congregation of the Church is always a mixture of the well, the sick, the rich, the poor, the mature, and the immature. It is the place where the ideal is preached and ministry is provided to the exception. It is a place where all are welcome.

In addition to programs that facilitated the rehabilitation of the individual, there were task forces of elders and members of the congregation that actively engaged the political community in dialogue to fashion solution-oriented programs for the various challenges facing the community. A political task force was organized to research and examine legislation and activities in the political community that affected the Church and the community. Politicians and other social leaders were often invited to discuss their programs with the leadership and before the congregation. The Church was indeed the evangelistic center of a region, but it was also the center of social and environmental change. The theology of the Kingdom of God was accompanied with practical strategies. Indeed, the Kingdom is not simply an expression, but it is an active influential power.

Church History

Since the person and ministry of the Holy Spirit is an integral to the Kingdom of God, something is to be said about the doctrine of the Holy Spirit as an experience of real power (Rom. 14:17). A brief review of Church history reveals the separation of the principle and practice of the Holy Spirit. Historically, the primitive Church is a charismatic community in which the Holy Spirit is the executive agent who administrates all things pertaining to the Church (John 16:7-11; 1 Cor. 12; Eph. 2:17-23, 4:3-7). In fact, it is the Holy Spirit that validates the ministry of the Church (Mark 16:15-18; Acts 15:6-8) and gives witness to the resurrection (Acts 2:32-33, 4:33); commissions ministers (Acts 1:4-8, 6:3-5, 13:1-4; Rom. 10:15; 1 Tim. 1:18, 4:14); facilitates evangelism (Acts 8:5-17, 29-38, 10:1-48); directs ministry (Acts 10:19-20, 44-47, 16:6-10); administers judgments (Acts 5:1-11, 15:6-11); adjusts prejudice (Acts 11:12-17); and gives prophetic warnings (Acts 11:27-28, 21:10-11). It is the Holy Spirit at work within the fixed liturgical structures that gives productive life to the corporate gathering of the Church community.

With the death of the early apostles and disciples, the Holy Spirit becomes less the object of experience and more the object of faith. The rise of false teachers and the infiltration of the Church with strange doctrines and heresies provide the need to reconsolidate the Church around some central authority and doctrine. In the late first and second centuries, there is an increasing concern for the details of rules, rights, and dogmas.[63] There is a corresponding decline of the interest in the relationship of the Church and the Holy Spirit.

Even though the primitive Church is almost exclusively a charismatic community with the Holy Spirit taking form in the "one Body of the exalted Christ," gradually the Holy Spirit is replaced with liturgical structures and other substitutes.[64] Direct inspiration of the Spirit becomes suspect. Since water baptism is regulated and faith and Spirit inspiration are not, the Spirit becomes more confined to the Church in Catholicism. Eventually, the Spirit becomes the possession of the Church and is associated with ritual acts. The bishop alone is authorized to bestow the Spirit.

The Protestant reaction to this ritualism and sacramental theology is to be seen in its emphasis in preaching and personal faith.[65] Authority is to be centered in the Bible and not in the Church. Faith is emphasized as being distinct and necessary prior to water-baptism, and water-baptism is subordinated to faith and the role of preaching. The Holy Spirit is viewed as the initiator of faith. Even though the activities of the Holy Spirit during the apostolic age are readily acknowledged, the Protestants assume the position that the "charismata" ceases with the apostles. The Spirit becomes subordinate to the Scriptures and the Scriptures take the place of the Catholic sacraments as the significant means of grace and inspiration. While the Catholics focus on the objectivity of the sacraments, the Protestants focus on the objectivity of the Scriptures. Although the Holy Spirit is considered the mediator in the work of salvation, He is not to be experienced apart

---

63 Unity and Diversity In The New Testament, *op. cit.*, p.351-362.

64 Ronald A. N. Kydd, *Charismatic Gifts in the Early Church: An Exploration Into the Gifts of the Spirit During the First Three Centuries of the Christian Church*, (Peabody, Ma.: Hendrickson Publishers, 1984).

65 William J. Bausch, *Pilgrim Church: A Popular History of Catholic Christianity*, (Mystic, Conn.: Twenty-Third Publications, 1989).

from the Scriptures. Therefore, conversion becomes essentially justification by faith alone.

The Pentecostals are against the rituals and sacramental emphasis of the Catholics and the intellectual orthodoxy of the Protestants. Subsequently, they focus their attention on the experience of the Holy Spirit. The Baptism in the Holy Spirit and the gifts of the Spirit are justified in the New Testament as being legitimate experiences in the lives of the earliest Christians (Acts 2:4; 4:31; 9:31; 10:44-46; 13:52; 19:6; Rom. 5:5; 8:1-16; 1 Cor. 12:7,13; 2 Cor. 3:6; 5:5; Gal. 4:6; 5:16-18, 25; I Thes. 1:5; Titus 3:6; John 3:8; 4:14; 7:38; 16:7). However, the Pentecostals separate the Spirit-baptism from the event of conversion-initiation and make the gift of the Spirit an experience, which follows after conversion. According to Paul and Luke, the Spirit is not something given subsequent to and distinct from becoming a Christian; nor is the Spirit only bestowed by an apostle or a bishop, or simply an experience restricted to the apostolic days.

Although the theological roots of the Cathedral of the Holy Spirit were in classical Pentecostalism, the Baptism of the Holy Spirit was viewed as an integral part of the conversion-initiation experience. As aforementioned, deliberate efforts were taken to demonstrate that the preaching of the Word and the administration of the sacraments of the Eucharist and water-baptism are not competing elements. The manifestation of the Holy Spirit in and through theologically informed saints is the welcomed and expected dimension of the corporate worship gathering. Furthermore, the administration of the baptism of the Holy Spirit as a present day phenomenon is also a responsibility of the priesthood of the believers. The believers and the leaders can "lay on hands" (Mark 16:18; Acts 13:3; 2 Tim. 1:6) and facilitate the baptism of the Holy Spirit, healing, and deliverance.

Historically, it is seen that the Holy Spirit does not dwell in "temples made with hand" (Acts 17:24). A scan of history of the Christian Church shows that worship takes place in catacombs, fields, in homes, by the river, in prisons, on ships, in automobiles, and even in airplanes. However, it is normal for believers to have a set place of worship.[66] These places of worship communicate something about the conviction of the people. For what we do in worship is expressed in the design and use of the building

---

66   Robert Webber, *Worship: Old and New* (Grand Rapids: Zondervan, 1992).

space. As aforementioned, this principle was demonstrated in the physical structure of the Cathedral.[67] The neo-gothic exterior with its interior choir lofts, baptismal founts, stained glass windows, padded pews, and all of the tapestries were an expression of the "liturgical" elements and an integration of the old and the new. In addition to the physical structures, there was the experience of the melodies and the songs of historic hymns; the contemporary gospels; the classical melodies; and spiritual songs all being delivered through choirs, special groups, and a full scale orchestra.

The opening of this section discusses the possibility of a "convergent theology," which influenced the attitude and behavior of the Church. A reformation model has been presented that represents a synthesis of the essentials of the Christian faith, both in theory and practice. The Cathedral of the Holy Spirit demonstrated an integration of the contributions of the diverse branches of the faith such as the Orthodox tradition with its liturgical and sacramental emphasis; the Reformed tradition with its emphasis on the centrality of Scriptures, justification by faith, and the universal priesthood; and the Pentecostal tradition with its emphasis on the Baptism of the Holy Spirit and its diverse ministration. This ministry also integrated the various polarities of the Kingdom of God into a system of practical and applied theology that provided outlets for the demonstrations of its concepts.

God still imparts principles and models of righteousness through the Church that must be proclaimed and demonstrated in the midst of a fragmented and confused world. Therefore, let His Kingdom come and let His will be done on earth as it is in heaven. Amen!

---

67 Kirby Clements, *A Philosophy of Ministry* (Decatur, Ga.: Clements Family Ministries 1993).

Conclusion and Summary

The Kingdom of God with all of its principles and power is the interpretative concept that defines reality, value, priority, authority, righteousness, joy, peace, and even evil. The conception and the misconception of the Kingdom of God influence the attitude and behavior of the redeemed community. The idea of the Kingdom of God is consistent throughout the Scripture with diversities of meanings and applications. The foundation of the Kingdom of God rest on the fact of God as Creator, Ruler, Organizer, and Maintainer of all creation. The dimensions of the Kingdom are redemptive and providential. God saves humanity and rules all creation. The crisis between the expectation and the realization of the Kingdom is resolved as we comprehend the progressive nature of revelation, the implications of symbols, types, and shadows, and the multiple polarities of meaning. The crisis after Pentecost represents human effort to interpret Biblical truths concerning the Kingdom of God and encapsulate those truths into practical meaning and application. It also represents the fact that all theology must be constantly evaluated for its agreement with Biblical truth. The significance of the Kingdom of God upon our worldview clearly reveals that God as Creator exerts an ongoing influence upon all aspects of human existence. It also demonstrates the implications of a proper worldview upon the socio-political processes of the world. The practical implications and the comparative analysis of different views of the Kingdom reveal a diversity of opinions regarding the Kingdom of God among the churches. While all the factions generated by this controversy agree on the existence of the Kingdom, they differ in their understanding of its nature, present implications, and time of its appearance. Finally, a local church model that demonstrates a convergence of theology and practice offers a tremendous example of effective ministry.

The following represents a summary of the chapters:

Chapter 1: The Idea of the Kingdom

1. It may be said that the whole of the preaching of Jesus Christ and the apostles is the Kingdom of God, and in the preaching of the Kingdom of God we are brought face to face with the whole of the revelation of God.

2. The Kingdom of God is the manifest rule and the expressed sovereignty of God and it is separate and distinct from any earthly ideology, philosophy, system, structure, organization, or form of government.

3. The principles and the power of the Kingdom of God are eternal and applicable to every generation, people, nation, and world.

4. The diversity of opinions regarding the Kingdom of God range from the view of a future hope, present spiritual blessing, an alternative society, a Utopian existence, the institutional church, to a political state.

5. The idea of the Kingdom is the connection between the Old and the New Testament and is prevalent in the preaching of the Lord Jesus, John Baptist, and the apostles.

6. The post-resurrection message of Jesus for forty days is the Kingdom of God.

7. The language of the Kingdom appears nine times in seven letters indicating its relation to Christian conduct and its significance to those redeemed out of every nation, kindred, tribe, and tongue.

8. The Kingdom is come in the incarnation, life, ministry, death, resurrection, and ascension of Jesus Christ.

9. The Kingdom is here as an experience in the Holy Ghost, its gifts, fruits, and the struggles against the flesh and the world; and the Kingdom is coming with the Second Coming of Christ when God will be all in all.

10. The fact that the rule of God is eternal and without restriction of time or geography; that the truths of the Kingdom endure throughout every generation regardless of the century; that the expectation of Old Testament prophets find fulfillment with the New Testament apostles and prophets; and that what is once declared to be a mystery becomes very clear, is the association between the Old Testament and the New Testament.

Chapter 2: The Foundation of the Kingdom

1. The creation motif is the basis for the government of God and the whole concept of His unlimited dominion and rule.

2. In creation God manifests Himself in mankind, establishes covenant, and delegates authority.

3. God's intention in creating Adam (male and female) is that they should multiply, fill the earth, subdue it, and bring all things under the government of God.

4. God never indicates that He will be passive or uninvolved with mankind or the creation.

5. Nations are sociological units created by God to compartmentalize humanity into manageable units over which He gives angelic oversight.

6. The management of nations is through the providential rule of God.

7. God imparts concepts of righteousness that may be demonstrated in institutions, organizations, and systems of human expressions such as economics, politics, commerce, science, entertainment, athletics, arts, and so forth.

8. The Kingdom of God is not restricted to religious matters but involves all areas of human existence.

9. Mankind is created in the image of God and equipped with the capacities of rationality, creativity, righteousness, and the power to rule over created things.

10. Mankind is not constituted to rule apart from God.

11. The major cause of disunity, disorder, disorientation, disease, and disaster in the world is due to fallen humanity seeking to govern itself without the counsel of God.

12. Sin is comprehensive in its domain and affects the spirit, soul, and body of mankind and also the entire creation.

13. Salvation is more comprehensive in reversing the effects of sin for it is the revelation and the restoration of Divine purposes, authority, and order.

14. The fulfillment of Divine purposes, authority, and order does not come through the literal annihilation of the earth but through the influential activities of the Holy Spirit working through an inspired, theologically informed, and obedient redeemed community.

15. Through the power of the Holy Spirit there are divine ideas, concepts, programs, and strategies imparted to redeemed humanity that serve as the foundation for institutions, organizations, policies, laws, governments, and relationships.

Chapter 3: The Dimensions of the Kingdom

1. The Kingdom of God is demonstrated in redemption and providence.

2. While salvation of the individual may be the center of God's will, it is not the circumference for His fullness is to fill all things.

3. Failure to comprehend the providential dimension of the Kingdom results in a preoccupation with the salvation of individuals at the expense of the knowledge and implication of God's rule in the affairs of the universe.

4. The providence of God exerts a moral influence over the agents of earthly government.

5. The world is not trees, hills, streams, or land but represents the government, institutions, organizations, laws, values, wisdom, knowledge, and lifestyles of fallen humanity seeking to discard God's government.

6. The concept that human existence is divided into sphere of the sacred (religions) and secular (athletics, politics, science, economics, entertainment, etc.) with the Kingdom of God being restricted to the religious sphere is erroneous.

7. Even thought the Kingdom of God is not defined by politics, economics, sociology, science, or any ideology, it is concerned with all spheres of human existence.

8. The principles and power of God are expressed in politics, science, economics, entertainment, athletics, and all areas of human welfare.

Chapter 4: The Expectation and the Realization of the Kingdom

1. The crisis of prophecy is the disparity that exists between the expectation and the realization of an anticipated idea.

2. The idea of the Kingdom of God is set forth in the Old Testament with its many symbols, types, and shadows.

3. The Old Testament prophets are "Messianic predictors" while the New Testament apostles and prophets are "Messianic clarifiers."

4. What the Old Testament prophets foretell and predict to come without a clear understanding, the New Testament apostles and prophets give the meaning and the understanding.

5. The Biblical idea of a mystery is a divine purpose that is hidden in the counsels of God and finally revealed at an appointed time to a particular people.

6. For the citizens of the Old Covenant, the Kingdom of God is anticipated as a single event in which the mighty manifestation of the power of God destroys the wicked kingdom of human rule and fills the earth with righteousness.

7. The Rabbinical expectation concerning the Kingdom of God is taken from the Old Testament references and includes the expectation of an age of plenty; an age of friendship; and end of pain; an age of peace; the supremacy of Israel; and the exaltation of Jerusalem.

8. The expectation of the Kingdom as being national, ethnic, and geographic indicates the extension of special privileges and responsibilities to a specific people, in a specific location, and at a specific time.

9. There is Biblical evidence that the prophets foretell a close and vital connection between Old Testament Israel and the New Testament Church indicating that the burden of the Old Testament prophecy is not limited to one ethnic people but to all nations.

10. Israel is used as a particular nation to bear witness to the revelation of God in the midst of universal idolatry; to demonstrate the benefits of covenant obedience to God; to receive, preserve, and transmit the Scripture; and to produce as to His humanity, the Lord Jesus Christ.

11. The New Testament reveals the connection and fulfillment of such terms as "nations of priests," "peculiar people," and the "Israel of God."

12. The Holy Spirit is not simply a "Pentecostal phenomena" that is peculiar to a radical group of people who shout, dance, speak in tongues, and prophesy but it is the norm of the Christian experience.

13. The Holy Spirit is the Executive Agent of the Kingdom of God and the Mediator of all earthly activities related to its existence and power.

14. The mystery of the Kingdom is the way that it is presently working with persuasion and subtle power.

15. The Gospels offer compelling evidence of how the appearance of the Messiah and the Kingdom in the life of the people in the time of Jesus does not correspond to Israel's hopes.

16. The standard of principle, practice, behavior, and belief in Israel's economy is supplanted by the coming of the Lord Jesus.

17. The fulfillment of anticipated promises concerning the Kingdom of God represents a "violent" departure from the Rabbinical concepts and anticipated hopes.

18. The apostles use language to demonstrate the close and vital connection which exist between the Old Testament Israel and the New Testament Church.

19. The New Testament reveals a fulfillment that is associated with terms such as "nations of priests," "peculiar people," "royal priesthood," "holy nations," and the "Israel of God."

20. The crisis of prophecy is demonstrated in the violent departure that the realized fulfillment assumes in reference to the expected fulfillment.

Chapter 5: Crisis After Pentecost

1. After Pentecost the apostles demonstrate the connection between the Kingdom of God and the person and ministry of the Holy Spirit among all people, nations, and tongues.

2. During the days of the apostles there is conflict between the expectation and the realization of promises that is due in part to the misunderstanding of the significance of the First Coming of Jesus Christ and the power and implication of the Holy Spirit.

3. There exists a diversity of post-Pentecostal interpretations of the Kingdom of God that range from it being a present reality, a future blessing, to an inner spiritual blessing.

4. Despite the diversity of opinions regarding the Kingdom, all the factions agree of the existence but disagree on the implications, dimensions, and time of its appearance.

5. The Kingdom is an inner spiritual blessing which is experienced only by way of the new birth, and yet is will involve the government of the nations of the world; it is a gift of God to be given in the future and yet it is received in the present; it is an inheritance which God will bestow upon His people when Christ comes again, and yet it is also a realm that believers enter now.

6. Despite the national, ethnic, or geographical associations, the Kingdom of God is the government of God and therefore is based upon the incarnation, life, ministry, death, and resurrection of the Lord Jesus Christ; which is introduced with power by the coming of the Holy Spirit; and which is extended throughout all nations of earth, and through all centuries of this era of grace by those who preach the gospel with the Holy Ghost sent down from above.

7. There are post-Pentecostal interpretations that relate the Kingdom of God to the institutional Church and view the growth and work of the Church as being synonymous with the Kingdom.

8. The Scripture offers a diversity of statements about the Kingdom of God as being a present reality, a future blessing, an inner spiritual blessing, and a future inheritance.

Chapter 6: The Kingdom of God and a Worldview

1. A worldview is the frame of reference that influences our attitudes, values, opinions, and behavior toward the world.

2. A productive worldview answers the critical questions of purpose, design, relationship, and the future such as: Why are we here?; Where are we going?; Who is in charge?; Can we change things?; Is there hope in the future?; How do we relate to other people.

3. The concept of the Kingdom of God addresses the intervention of God in human affairs; the revelation and restoration of divine purposes and intentions; and human response to such divine knowledge in the forms of organizations, institutions, laws, governments, economics, and all systems of human relationships.

4. The two prevalent worldviews influenced by concepts of the Kingdom of God are theism and deism which differ in the nature of God and the degree of His involvement in the ongoing activity of the world.

5. Deism presents God as creator who exerts no ongoing influence on people or the world, while theism presents God as Creator and as being personal and continually involved in the affairs of the universe.

6. The theistic worldview defines the meaning of such terms as "influence," "transform," "occupy," "disciple," and "leaven" that are specifically associated with the Great Commission.

7. A Biblical worldview express the difference between "escape" and "engagement;" demonstrates the belief that God is involved with humanity; that Divine plans and strategies are known; and eliminates the boundary line between the "sacred" and the "secular."

Chapter 7: Practical Implications

1. Perceptions of the Kingdom of God are translated into principles, practices, and priorities that ultimately function as the interpretative concept that influences the life and activities of the church in the areas of its infrastructures, evangelism, outreach ministries, coalitions, and associations with other local churches.

2. When the Kingdom is interpreted to be "not of this world," spiritual, and relegated totally to the future, then the ministry of the local church neglects any concern for the present socio-political welfare of the community and regards the disintegration of the community and even the world as a sign of God's judgment.

3. A local church influenced by the "other world" concept of the Kingdom will make very little effort to influence politicians, educators, and other cultural architects who direct the welfare of the community since the Kingdom is not viewed as being involved with such "carnal matters."

4. If individual evangelism is viewed as the chief responsibility of the church, priority is given to the numerical growth of the local church and the kinds of ministry programs that attracts and keeps members.

5. If the grace of God is seen not to operate in the spheres of the arts, science, technology, entertainment, education, or athletics, then the church with its preaching, teaching, and outreach ministry becomes a "cultural critic" rather than a "cultural architect."

6. The Church and the Kingdom are distinct in that the Kingdom relates to laws, rules, and legislation, while the Church relates to meetings, worship, and congregations.

7. The Church is the redeemed community serving as the executive representative of the power, principles, priorities, and practices of the Kingdom.

8. The government of God exerts its influence in redemption (individual salvation) and providence (cosmic order).

Chapter 8: Comparative Analysis of Different Views

1. All views of the Kingdom of God agree on its existence, but differ in their expressions of its nature, present implications, and time of its appearance.

2. The Kingdom is viewed as either being future hope, present spiritual blessings, an alternative society, the Church, or some transformed state of social existence to be anticipated.

3. The Kingdom of God as future, spiritual, and heavenly puts emphasis on the Second Coming of Jesus Christ as a future hope; a final judgment with the literal annihilation of the present heaven and earth; the formation of a "new heaven and a new earth;" the culmination of all evil and injustice; and the formation of a new creation (utopia) in which all the earth experiences peace, holiness, and happiness.

4. The Kingdom of God as present, physical, and earthly makes no distinction between the Church and the Kingdom; views the visible, militant, triumphant, and institutional Church upon the earth in every generation as the Kingdom; proposes that fair government and just social structures are possible through the progressive rule of Christians in all areas of life; and that the Kingdom is a culture that is transformed by humanity organized according to the will of God.

5. The Kingdom of God as present, future, spiritual, natural, earthly, and heavenly represents a convergence, with modifications, of different polarities of views.

6. The convergent view of the Kingdom views the world in need of a message, a model, and demonstration of what righteousness, peace, and joy really are in the Holy Ghost.

7. The convergent view sees the Kingdom and the Church as separate and distinct entities with the Church called to influence the activities of the world through the proclamation and demonstration of the principles of the Kingdom.

8. The convergent view comprehends the depravity of sin; the necessity of spiritual regeneration; the need for solution-oriented programs; the necessity for collaboration with authorities in every area of human existence; and the commission to preach the gospel with the power and manifestation of the Holy Spirit.

Chapter 9: A Convergent Model

1. A classical Pentecostal/Charismatic Church experienced a radical transformation in its theology and practices and demonstrated a convergence of the five-fold ministry, Holy Spirit dynamic, expressive worship, liturgy, and socially active ministry programs.

2. The Cathedral of the Holy Spirit was a multi-cultural congregation that worshiped God in psalms, hymns, spirituals songs, and makes melodies in their hearts.

3. The Cathedral demonstrated the implication of Kingdom theology upon the church architecture and ministry in the construction of a neo-gothic Cathedral.

4. The idea of the Kingdom of God as a future hope and the Church as a colony of redeemed people awaiting their deliverance form this present world is transformed by a fresh revelation of the Kingdom of God and the finished work of Jesus Christ.

5. Fresh revelatory meaning was given to such phrases as "thy kingdom come, they will be done on earth as it is in heaven" and "held in the heaven until the restitution of all things."

6. Attention was given to words such as "witness," "occupy," "disciple," "salt," and "light."

7. The Church is not a "cultural critic" that denounces the problems of war, crime, immorality, and disorganization of the world.

8. The Church is a "cultural architect" empowered by the Holy Spirit to offer solutions through the proclamation and demonstrations of the principles of the Kingdom of God.

9. A theology of escape is exchanged for a theology of influence and the boundary line between the sacred and the secular is erased.

10. Theological concepts and companion strategies are blended together in the development of stewardship responsibilities in areas of law, politics, education, science, athletics, entertainment, and commerce.

11. The Cathedral reconciled the three major streams of Christian traditions (Reformed, Orthodox, and Pentecostal) through patterns and models of worship and ministry.

12. The practical influence of the principles of the Kingdom of God is expressed in the development of a ministry philosophy.

13. The Church must preach and demonstrate the ideal of the purposes and intentions of God for a contemporary world of people, institutions, organizations, governments, and laws, while ministering to the very individuals and systems that fall short of that ideal.

14. The doctrine of the Holy Spirit is inseparable from the theology and practice of the Kingdom of God.

In conclusion, let it be said that if the whole of the preaching of Jesus Christ and His apostles is the Kingdom of God, and in the preaching of the Kingdom of God we are brought face to face with the whole of the revelation of God, then we are not thinking and preaching correctly if we are not focusing on the Kingdom of God. If the Kingdom is the essential reference and if it is not separate and distinct from the life, ministry, death, resurrection, ascension, and enthronement of Jesus and the coming of the Holy Spirit, then there can be no effective ministry without the proclamation and demonstration of its principles, power, and practices. However, it is also sure, that misconceptions regarding the nature, dimensions, present implications, and future expectations of the Kingdom exert tremendous influence upon the life and activities of the Church. Let us understand it right; let us preach and teach it right; let us demonstrate it right; and the world will glorify Him whose right it is to rule! Amen!

CPSIA information can be obtained at www.ICGtesting.com
Printed in the USA
LVOW07s1035120216

474834LV00002B/4/P